To my coaches, teammates, officials, players, and players' parents.

Table of Contents

Preface

Indoor Soccer Strategies and Tactics is for coaches and players of all ages. Indoor soccer continues to grow rapidly in all areas of North America, yet there is very little written on the subject.

This book is intended to help individuals, coaches, and teams increase their knowledge of the game and to increase their skills at indoor soccer. As individuals and teams improve, the leagues in which they play begin to improve dramatically. So whether you are a player trying to improve your skills, or a coach looking to take a team to higher levels of play, this book is for you.

This book is not about basic soccer skills. It assumes the reader has a basic knowledge of outdoor soccer skills such as dribbling, passing, and shooting. There are numerous books that cover these skills in detail with tips, drills, and instruction. This book covers the aspects of indoor soccer that are *different* from outdoor soccer—and there are many. In fact, the differences are so numerous and dramatic that it is not a stretch to say that indoor and outdoor soccer are two entirely different sports.

We will discuss the important differences between indoor and outdoor soccer, and cover systems and strategies for both offense and defense for indoor

1

soccer. We will analyze the transition game, strategies for substitution, goal keeping, and special plays. Finally, we will cover some drills that are specifically designed to practice indoor soccer skills.

By the time you finish this book, you will have a much greater understanding of the intricacies of the game. You should also have the knowledge to become a much better player and/or coach.

I have been playing and coaching outdoor and indoor soccer for more than 36 years. As of this writing, I play for two different indoor teams and have coached more than two dozen indoor and outdoor teams. I have learned the strategies and tactics by watching, playing with, and interviewing some of the best players and teams in the game.

Most players that play indoor soccer started playing outdoor soccer first. These players often attempt to bring their outdoor knowledge and skills and apply them to the indoor game, but many find that their knowledge and skills don't convert to indoor as easily as they might have thought. However, I have found that once they realize how different indoor soccer is from outdoor soccer, and once they employ the strategies and tactics provided in this book, they can radically transform their performances in indoor soccer in a short period of time. I hope you and your team can benefit as well.

Warning: I must let you know that I started playing indoor soccer while I was playing on an outdoor team. I played on both for a few seasons, but soon realized I enjoy indoor soccer much more. The same thing has happened to several people I play with. Beware! The same thing could happen to you. Whatever the outcome, let's dive in and learn about indoor soccer!

Author's note: For the diagrams in this book, we will have two teams: Home and Visitors. The Home team is always represented by black dots defending the goal on the left side of the page, and the Visitors are represented by white dots defending the goal on the right side of the page. By keeping the teams the same color and oriented the same way throughout the book, it is easier to transfer the discussion from offense to defense and back again. For the purposes of this book, we will assume that the reader is always on the Home team and the Visitors are always the opponents. The keeper is shown as a smaller circle to differentiate him or her from the other players.

Chapter 1: Introduction

Indoor soccer is fast paced, fun to watch, and fun to play. Indoor facilities are opening up in every area of North America, particularly in northern regions and Canada. Year round play, extended hours, and no weather cancellations add to the sport's growing popularity.

Interest in professional indoor soccer has ebbed and flowed over the past 125 years. The United States Indoor Soccer Association reports that the first official game was in 1885 in a roller skating rink. It wasn't until 1923 that the first indoor league was formed. Since then, more than a dozen professional leagues have come and gone. Apparently this was not due to lack of spectator attendance; some leagues averaged between 10,000 and 20,000 spectators per game. Those attendance numbers are not significantly different from today's National Hockey League numbers. The complete history of indoor soccer can be found at the United States Indoor Soccer Association's website at www.usindoor.com.

The Rules of Indoor Soccer

One result of the number of different leagues in the history of indoor soccer is the variation in the rules of play. As of this writing, there are several versions of the rules of play, or laws, for indoor soccer. Three common sets of rules are:

- United States Indoor Soccer Association rules found at www.usindoor.com
- Major Indoor Soccer League rules found at http://www.misl.net/upload_images/mislrules06.pdf
- U.S. Soccer Federation Futsal Laws of the Game found at www.ussoccer.com.

Interestingly, all of the rules state that the rules vary by location. The size of the field, or pitch, can vary as well.

For players and coaches new to indoor soccer but familiar with outdoor soccer, the following rules are different from outdoor soccer but common to most indoor facilities:

- The ball cannot cross all three lines in the air. This is called the three line rule and if it occurs, the ball is brought back to the defensive zone and a free kick is given to the attacking team from the spot on the yellow or red line. This is roughly equivalent to icing in hockey.
- There is no rule for being offside. The three line rule diminishes the advantage of "cherry picking."
- Substitution is on the fly and is unlimited. Some locations require that a player come off before

another can go on to the field. Other locations allow players to come on to the field as long as they don't interfere with the play, as in ice hockey.

- Minor infractions trigger free kicks as in outdoor soccer. More flagrant infractions draw a two minute penalty where the offending player is sent off the field resulting in a power play scenario.

Indoor Soccer Facilities

One of the reasons for the differences in rules is that facilities vary greatly from location to location. Fields are different sizes and the lines are painted differently on virtually every field. Fields often differ in size due to physical constraints. For example, many indoor facilities are converted from warehouses, factories, industrial buildings, shopping centers, or other pre-existing buildings. The size of a field may be driven by the amount of space available. Some leagues play in gymnasiums.

Indoor facilities are becoming more common in northern regions where the weather prohibits outdoor play much of the year. Also, it appears that once indoor soccer catches on in an area, other facilities and leagues grow. Many metropolitan areas have numerous indoor facilities. It is common to see indoor soccer facilities combined with other indoor sports and recreation such as lacrosse, basketball, hockey, roller skating, batting cages, dance studios, swimming facilities, and many others. The United States Indoor Soccer Association website www.ussoccer.com has 758 indoor facilities listed in the United States and Canada as of this writing. Several more are under construction.

The United States Indoor Soccer Association reports that there are 4.8 million people playing indoor soccer, making it the ninth most popular team sport in America. Outdoor soccer is third behind basketball and baseball.

This book covers strategies and tactics applicable to indoor soccer no matter what the size of the field is or what the rules are for a particular location. Anyone playing indoor soccer can benefit from the information presented here.

Who is playing indoor soccer?

Many outdoor teams join indoor leagues to stay in shape and practice in their off seasons. Children of all ages play, and adults who cannot play sports on weekends find playing later on a weeknight, sometimes past midnight, easier on their schedules.

No matter where it is played, indoor soccer is on the rise. Chapter three covers the similarities and differences between indoor and outdoor soccer. Perhaps after studying the differences, it will become clearer why indoor soccer is growing.

Chapter 2: Field of Play

The indoor soccer field, or pitch, varies by location. A typical field is 200 feet by 85 feet, but can be anywhere from 120 feet to 215 feet long by 50 to 100 feet wide. The variation in size allows the game to be played in a variety of locations ranging from a school gymnasium to a professional arena.

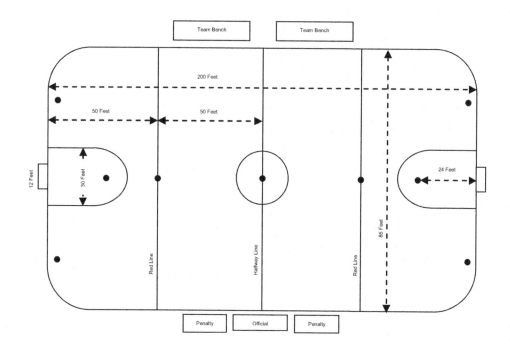

Exhibit 2-1

The diagram of a basic field is shown in Exhibit 2-1. Fields are different in many ways particularly in the delineation of the penalty areas. However, the characteristics of most fields are:

- There are three lines separating the zones. The lines at either end are normally yellow or red.
- Goals are 12 to 14 feet wide and 6 ½ to 8 feet high.
- Goals are recessed into the end walls.
- The penalty area may be rectangular, semi-circular, or a combination.
- There may or may not be separate penalty boxes or benches for players to sit while serving penalty time.
- Walls, or dasher boards, can range from 3 ½ feet to 8 feet in height. The boards are higher above the goals.
- Playing surface may be concrete, wood floors, one layer of artificial grass, an advanced system of padding and artificial turf, or other surfaces. Most facilities have turf of some kind.
- The center circle typically has a radius of 15 feet.

Chapter 3: Comparison to Outdoor

While indoor soccer and outdoor soccer have many things in common, it is not a stretch to say that they are entirely different sports. The similarities are roughly equivalent to the similarities between tennis and racquetball. Tennis and racquetball both require the players to hit a ball with a racquet. Likewise, indoor and outdoor soccer both require kicking a ball with your feet. Beyond this, the differences become greater than the similarities. In fact, the strategies and tactics in indoor soccer resemble those used in ice hockey more than they resemble tactics used in outdoor soccer. It is my experience that many people coaching or playing indoor soccer started playing outdoor soccer first. So before we cover the strategies and tactics of indoor soccer, let's take a look at the differences between indoor and outdoor soccer.

The significant differences between indoor and outdoor soccer are listed below. In indoor soccer:

The walls, or dasher boards, keep the ball in play more.

While there are stoppages in play in indoor soccer, they are far fewer than in outdoor play. This is perhaps the biggest difference between indoor and outdoor soccer and it changes the game dramatically. Virtually everything about the game is affected, including the tempo of play, tactics, substituting, goal keeping, and more. We will cover all of these in detail.

The field is significantly smaller.

Indoor field sizes vary from location to location, but a typical size is 200 feet by 85 feet. This is the same size as a hockey rink. Some are significantly smaller. A 200 x 85 foot indoor field is about a quarter the size of a full size outdoor field. The number of players on an indoor field is usually about half the number on a full size field, therefore the players have about half as much room to maneuver. Looking at it a different way, there are twice as many people per square foot of field space in indoor soccer. When there is less room to play, the game becomes more compact. The players are closer together all the time and no one is ever very far from the action. This affects every aspect of the game.

There is also a roof. Some facilities have a ceiling as low as 18 feet. This inhibits long, lofting passes. When a ball hits the ceiling, it is considered out of bounds at that point.

The game is much faster.

A smaller field makes the game more compact and speeds up play. Transitions occur from attacking to defending very quickly, and they often change back again immediately. For example, in outdoor soccer, it is not often that a shot on goal is answered with a shot on goal at the other end of the field within in a few seconds. In indoor soccer, this can happen several times in a game. A hard, inaccurate shot on goal can bounce off the back wall and go back more than half the length of the field without being touched, possibly creating an immediate breakaway.

Players must make decisions much more quickly.

In outdoor play, the transitions can take time to develop and the players have more space (and consequently more time) to formulate and execute strategy. In indoor play, control of the ball often must be with one touch, since the opposing players are usually in very close proximity. This means players need to be able to adapt to the situation quickly, and many teams find that with less time to set up they talk more and call more audible plays. For experienced teams, there is constant chatter on the field between players.

There is less open field dribbling.

Open field dribbling is less common in indoor soccer for two reasons. First, the dribbler typically gets attacked quickly since defenders are usually very close by. Second, it doesn't take long to dribble from one end of the field to the other. Outdoor teams with star dribblers don't always make great transitions to indoor play.

There is less room for error.

Because the field is smaller and the players are closer together, errors are magnified. For example, in outdoor soccer, a mid-air trap may land a few feet beside or in front of the trapper, and he or she may have room to recover it before being challenged. In indoor soccer, the proximity of the opposing players makes even the smallest mistakes easier to challenge. One thing to keep in mind is that the ball tends to bounce higher in indoor soccer compared to an outdoor grass field. Teams coming indoors sometimes have trouble trapping or passing when getting used to the surface.

Another example of common errors is passing. Passing in indoor soccer must be much more accurate, again due to the constraints of the field and proximity of opposing players. Passes that are not perfectly timed are very often taken by the other team. One touch passes become critical, and their accuracy must be very good. Once a team gets accustomed to this, it is not unusual for players to string multiple one touch passes together in an offensive push.

There is much more shooting.

In outdoor soccer, the number of shots on goal may be five or fewer per side per game. In indoor, it is not uncommon to have 50 or more shots on goal per side. This is another result of the smaller field. Shots can come at any time and from any position. While it is not common for goal keepers to score at the other end of the field, it is common for keepers to assist in goals by making timely and accurate feeds up-field.

In indoor soccer, as in hockey, defenders often shoot and score. Therefore, all of the players on the field in indoor soccer are often all-around players. Many defenders move up-field on an offensive push and become offensive players in a high pressure situation. This is also similar to shooting guards in basketball. We will cover this later.

There is much more scoring.

More shooting means more scoring and indoor games often have scores in double digits. Some facilities have added a three point line at 45 feet from the center of the goal. Shots made from outside this line are three points and shots made from inside are two points. With this scoring system, teams can score more than 20 points in a game. However, most recreational indoor leagues count one goal as one point.

There are rebound shots.

In indoor soccer, as we have discussed, there are many more shots on goal. Some of these shots come from rebounds off the back wall. In outdoor soccer, if the shooter misses wide or high, the play stops and the keeper gets a long kick downfield. In indoor, the ball stays in play and there may be multiple shots on goal until the keeper gets possession, the ball goes out of play high, or the defense gets control. There could be a half dozen or more shots before one of these events occurs.

Rebound shots can be opportunistic or they can be planned. In either scenario, the offensive players in front of the goal must have very quick reflexes and fast decision making ability to make the rebound shots. One touch control is extremely important. Passing off the back wall is very effective and it is one of the most difficult situations for the goal keeper to defend against.

Passes are different.

Long passes are inhibited by the roof as we discussed. Long passes are also inhibited by the three line rule. That rule states that the ball cannot pass all three lines on the field (both red lines and the midfield line). This is similar to icing in hockey. Long, high crossing passes from the wings are not possible because there is not enough room for a pass to get up in the air from the corners and get back down in the area in front of the goal. Similarly, corner kicks are very close to the goal and are not the high lofting type seen outdoors.

So passes are much shorter and must be more accurate. On breakaways, passes need to be passed into the space in front of the pass receiver, but not too far ahead. When a receiver is standing still (not recommended) the ball must be passed to the receiver's proper foot to allow the next pass to be a one touch pass or a good trap. See comments about less room for error above.

Positions overlap more.

In indoor soccer, defensive players often make runs to the opposing goal in a high pressure offense, which we will cover later, or in a breakaway situation. In a breakaway case, a midfielder or forward may drop back to cover the defensive position for the advancing defender.

Left and right positions are also less defined. Players cross the field with regularity, and they are constantly moving from left to right and back again. During a shift, a midfielder may play up, back, left, and right, and if she is fast enough, she may never be caught out of position.

Substitution is on the fly.

Substitution is constant, as it is in hockey. This makes the game very dynamic and keeps the game moving. Substitutions can occur at stoppages, such as when the ball goes out of play. Keep in mind, though, that in indoor play, the players don't have to travel anywhere near the distance they do when substituting in outdoor play. So even when there are substitutions on stoppages in indoor soccer, they take up less time than they do in outdoor play.

Substitution is also unlimited. Players usually have numerous shifts per game. Players may be part of a line shift, like in hockey. In recreational play, players often take themselves out when they get tired. In this case, they may come off as a single.

In outdoor soccer, a player may stay on the field for an entire half, or even most of a game. In recreational indoor soccer, players rarely go past five minutes if they are running hard. In professional indoor soccer, a shift may last two minutes or less. However, indoor soccer players will typically get back on the field for another shift very quickly after coming off.

There is less downtime.

There are far fewer instances where the ball goes out of bounds in indoor soccer. This is particularly true for younger players. They may not have developed their skills enough to consciously keep the ball in bounds in outdoor play, and they may not have the power to get the ball over the boards in indoor play. Adult indoor players who realize the value in short, accurate passes and accurate shooting also contribute to keeping the ball in play more than in outdoor soccer.

Keeping the ball in play leads to less downtime. When the ball does go out of play or when there is stoppage for a penalty or score, the setup time is significantly less in indoor soccer. This is because the ball is retrieved and placed more quickly (it is usually not far away) and the players don't have as far to travel to reset for the next play. This might not sound like an important factor, but players transitioning from outdoor to indoor often find that the ball is back in play much more quickly.

There are power plays.

In outdoor soccer, a player may be awarded a yellow card which does not change the dynamics of the game. He or she may receive a red card, in which case he or she is ejected from the game. In indoor soccer, there are minor infractions which result in free kicks, but more serious infractions result in power plays.

Power plays in indoor soccer are similar to power plays in hockey where a player comes off for a short period of time, typically for two minutes. That player's team must play one person short for the duration of the penalty, or until the opposing team scores. This has a greater effect on the game than when an outdoor team must play a player short. The reason for this is straightforward: if the normal number of field players in indoor is usually five (not including the keeper), a loss of a person puts the team down by 20% of its players. In outdoor, a one person reduction from a team playing ten field players (not including the keeper) is 10%.

Fitness level required is different.

Indoor soccer requires players to be very physically fit, just as in outdoor soccer. However, the type of fitness is different. Many players transitioning from outdoor soccer find that they get tired or winded much more quickly in indoor soccer.

I was sitting outside the glass at a game when someone sat down next to me that had never seen indoor soccer played before. He commented that it looks easier than outdoor soccer because the field is smaller. Often, spectators or parents that have never played also believe this. I smiled and told him that the game is much harder and more physically taxing.

The main reason for this is the combination of the shorter downtime periods and the smaller field size. These factors combined together mean that players are almost always in the play and there is very little recovery time between sprints. It often takes three or four games before players get accustomed to this difference. Players who run long distances to stay in shape for soccer need to transition to sprint oriented runs and exercises to get maximum benefit for indoor soccer.

It's more fun to watch.

Perhaps this is opinion and not an actual difference between indoor and outdoor soccer. However, many of the differences noted here make indoor more exciting, specifically:

- The game is faster
- There is less room for error
- There is more shooting
- There are rebound shots
- There is more scoring

More action and more scoring make indoor soccer a blast to watch. These factors make the game more fun to play as well.

Major Indoor Soccer League evidently recognized that spectators like action and scoring, so they added the three point line to make scores even higher. The National Hockey League and the National Football League also recognized that North American spectators like scoring and changed their rules to encourage more scoring. As more people play and discover the differences from outdoor soccer, indoor soccer may once again draw tens of thousands of spectators to arenas across North America.

Chapter 4: Game Systems and Strategies

System formations

Indoor soccer is played with five, six, or seven players on the field at a time per team, including a goal keeper. Adults usually play five on five plus a keeper, and youth teams typically play six on six plus a goal keeper.

A game system is how the players are organized on the field. Let's start with adults playing five on five. For five on five play, there are three popular systems. Probably the most common is the 2-1-2 shown in Exhibit 4-1 where F=Forward, M=Midfielder, and D=Defender:

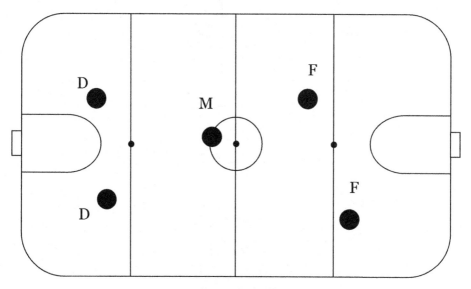

Exhibit 4-1

Teams using the 2-1-2 system must have a very capable midfielder to play the position alone. This player must be very fast, very fit, and very skillful. The midfielder can move up quickly to help the forwards with 3-man quick breaks.

Some teams play a 2-2-1 system as shown in Exhibit 4-2 below:

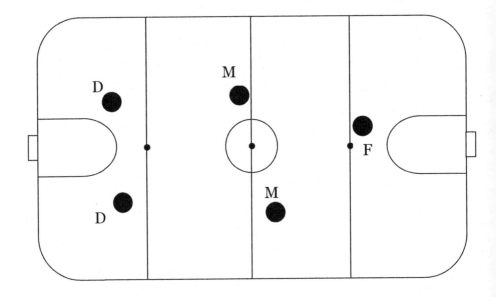

Exhibit 4-2

The 2-2-1 system is a defensive system useful for playing against teams with a superior offense or faster forwards. The extra help in the middle of the field helps the defense get set quicker than if two forwards get caught on the attacking end of the field. This system is good for teams with average speed or players that are still improving on their indoor soccer fitness levels.

In this system, the lone forward, sometimes called the target player, will often be breaking downfield alone. If this forward is exceptionally fast, he or she may be able to get past the defense for 1 v 0 breakaways against the opposing keeper. This forward must be a superior ball handler and finisher because he or she may be frequently rebounding his or her own shots.

Some teams play a 2-3 system as shown in Exhibit 4-3 below:

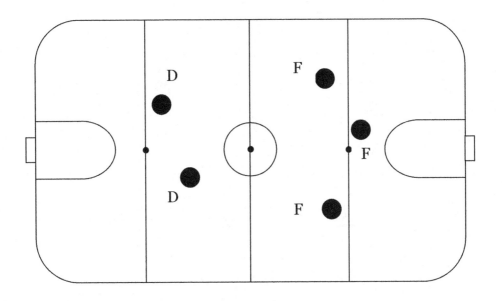

Exhibit 4-3

The 2-3 system is occasionally used on shorter fields. On a short field, say 120-150 feet, there might not be enough room to deploy midfielders. This is effective if the offense is superior to the opposing defense.

One drawback to this system is that the offensive players may all think someone else will travel back to help the defense. This can lead to a 3 v 2 or 4 v 2 situation for the defense.

Many leagues have the younger players play six on six. For six person systems, there are two main choices: 2-2-2 or 3-3.

The 2-2-2 looks like this:

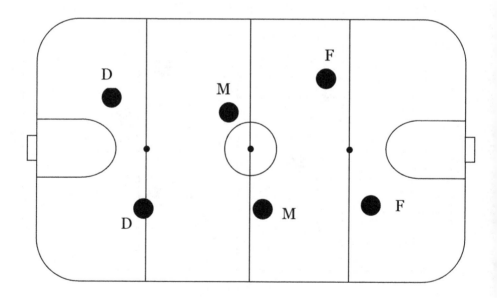

Exhibit 4-4

The 2-2-2 system is a great system for youth players playing six on six. It is very flexible and provides redundancy for the positions on the field. It is particularly effective if all of the players are good passers. Deliberate movement of the players can create continuous passing options which can frustrate the opposing defense. This system is often superior to the 3-3 system.

Even though the 2-2-2 system is usually superior, many coaches deploy a 3-3 system as shown in Exhibit 4-5 below:

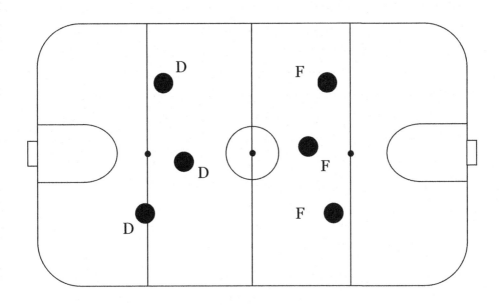

Exhibit 4-5

The 3-3 system is effective on shorter fields where a midfield may get too crowded.

The danger of the 3-3 system is the same as a 2-3 system: the forwards all believe someone else will drop back to help the defense. If a defender gets caught too far up, or if the opposition plays a 2-2-2 with the midfielders pressing forward, there is a good chance of an odd man rush (an attack with a superior number of players) overwhelming the defense.

When a team employs a 3-3 system, it is often easy to see a large gap between the two lines in the center of the field. Younger players who have been taught to stay in position on defense don't come far enough forward to take command of the middle third of the field, and the forwards, eager to score, wait in the attacking end of the field for the defense to clear the ball up to them. This method of having the defense clear the ball up to the forwards might have some limited success in outdoor play, but it often leads to three line violations in indoor play.

For the purposes of consistency, we will use five field players per team in the diagrams for the rest of this book. However, the information can be used and applied no matter how many players are on the field.

System strategies

There are two main system strategies: high pressure and low pressure.

High Pressure Strategy

A high pressure strategy is similar to a full court press in basketball. It is also similar to a fore-checking scenario in hockey when the defenders come up into the attacking end of the ice to put pressure on the opposing team.

When a team has possession of the ball in a high pressure attack, the team keeps passing in the attacking third of the field until someone gets a clear shot. If the opposing team has the ball, the high pressure strategy pressures the other team to make mistakes in their own end. This is effective against a team that has trouble making accurate passes. The added pressure makes poor passing even more detrimental.

Outdoor teams making the transition to indoor may not be accustomed to their defensive players being attacked with the ball. In outdoor soccer, if a defender wins the ball, other players often begin retreating back down the field in expectation of a long pass or clearing kick by the defensive player. In a high pressure strategy in indoor soccer, defensive players have to pass their way out of their own end. They should never try to dribble their way out.

When a team is pressuring the opponents in their own end, they need to keep them away from the walls and force them to pass back to the center of the field as shown in Exhibit 4-6:

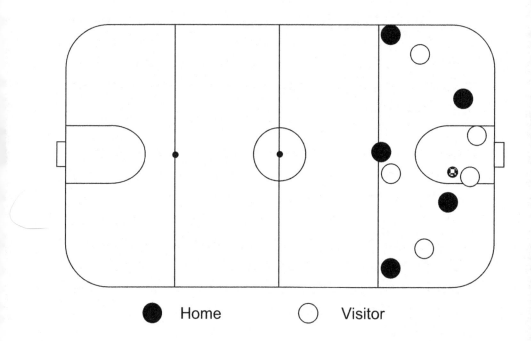

● Home   ○ Visitor

Exhibit 4-6

In a high pressure strategy, the attacking team (Home team in this example) must have very quick defenders. They must be able to drop back quickly and pick up a quick breakaway. The danger for the Home team in this scenario is over-committing. If one of the players over-commits and is beaten, there will be a breakaway resulting in an odd man rush.

A modified version of the high pressure system is when the defenders press past midfield, but not all the way past the opponents' red line. It is similar to the high pressure strategy, but gives the Home defensive players a little more room to react if the opposing team breaks away. The modified high pressure system is shown in Exhibit 4-7:

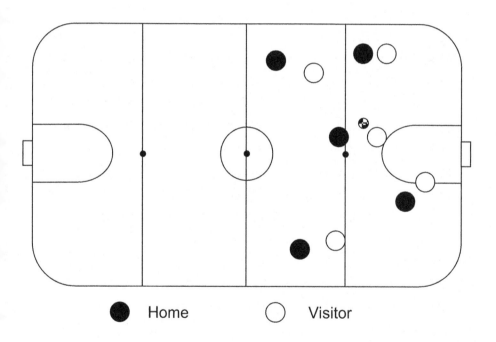

●   Home   ○   Visitor

Exhibit 4-7

Notice that the Home team is blocking the access to the walls. They must try to keep the ball in the center of the field to create shooting opportunities if they get a quick turnover. Similarly, if they have moved from their own end with the ball and they utilize the modified high pressure system in the formation above, they should work the ball toward the middle to create shooting opportunities.

Notice also that no Visitor team player is behind a Home team player. If the Visitor team leaves a cherry picker at midfield, the Home team must cover or be ready for a fast counter attack.

The high pressure strategy can be very effective at frustrating an opposing team, no matter which team has the ball. The Visitor team will find it difficult to get out of its own end if all five Home players are pressing in. Visitor forwards will have to drop back and help to avoid a collapse of the defense. If the forwards have to drop back deep to help on a regular basis, they will get much more tired than normal, and will have to make longer sprints when counter-attacking.

The high pressure strategy works well for teams that are very fast and very fit. If only one person cannot keep up, the entire system breaks down, because there will be a man disadvantage if the Visitor team can pull out fast enough.

Low Pressure Strategy

A low pressure strategy is a more conservative strategy, and it is also more common. A low pressure strategy is more defensive in nature. It keeps the defenders in their own end and helps offset a fast break from becoming problematic for the defense. A low pressure strategy by the Home team is shown in Exhibit 4-8.

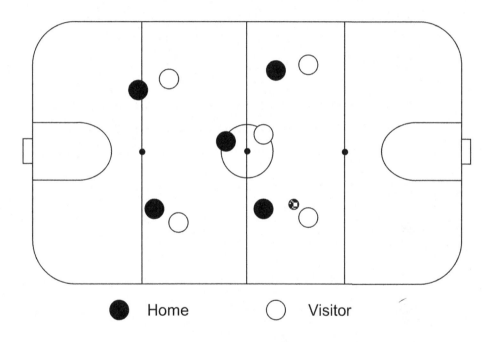

● Home   ○ Visitor

Exhibit 4-8

In Exhibit 4-8, notice that the Home team still has all of the Visitor team covered. Notice also that the Home team defenders have moved to toward the middle of the field in an attempt to drive the Visitor team outside toward the walls. The two Home forwards must stay in front of the Visitor defenders. If the Visitor team deploys a high pressure system, the Home forwards will have to drop back into their own third of the field to defend.

The low pressure strategy is helpful in defending against teams with fast forwards executing strong fast breaks. If the Visitor team pushes forward with a high pressure attack and the Home team does not force a turnover, the Home team will have no choice but to drop back into its own end to defend.

If the Visitor team plays a low pressure strategy when it has the ball, then the setup looks like Exhibit 4-9:

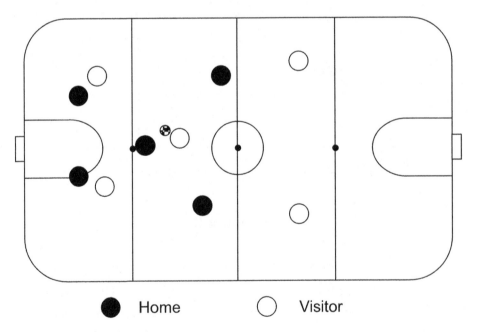

● Home   ○ Visitor

Exhibit 4-9

The Home team forwards can wait for a turnover and fast break, or they can drop back and help on defense if needed.

While the high pressure strategy is more like strategies used in basketball or hockey, the low pressure strategy is more like outdoor soccer where the defenders stay back on their own end of the field.

They systems and strategies a team selects will depend on its own skill level and the expected or known skill levels of its opponents.

Chapter 5: Offense

In the discussion of offensive tactics specific to indoor soccer, we will cover three areas: passing and dribbling; attack scenarios; and shooting.

Passing and Dribbling

As we covered earlier, passing and dribbling are different in indoor soccer than they are for outdoor soccer. Passing and dribbling tactics are as follows:

Tactic: Dribble less

The indoor field is smaller than the outdoor field, as we have seen. There is dramatically less open space where a player can carry the ball for ten, twenty, or thirty yards at a time without being challenged. Outdoor players and skilled dribblers will find that they are challenged much more quickly and much more often in indoor play due to the proximity of the defending players. Unless the opposition is playing very conservatively, a player with the ball should expect to be challenged immediately upon receiving the ball. Therefore, players need to be ready to pass the ball the instant they get it. This means all the players need to know where their teammates are or will be at all times.

39

Tactic: Know when to dribble

The preceding tactic, dribble less, does not mean don't dribble at all. There are times not to dribble, but there are times when it makes sense to dribble. The time to dribble is when a player has the ball and is 1 v 1 with the last defender or 1 v 0 on a fast break. In these scenarios, the upside to success is greater than the downside to failure. Waiting for support in either of these set ups gives the defense time to get back and defend.

In a 1 v 1 scenario, it makes sense to take on the last defender in order to get a shot on goal. This is most likely in the middle third of the field or in the attacking end. In the event the dribbler loses the ball, there will be room to transition back to defense and there will be other players on his or her team to help get the ball back.

Tactic: Keep the end in mind

Keep in mind that there are only two desired outcomes from dribbling: a shot on goal or a successful pass. That's it. If it is doubtful that either of these will occur after trying to dribble, don't do it.

Tactic: Pass quickly and accurately

There is no room in indoor soccer for sloppy or inaccurate passes. The space is too confined and the players are too close together. In outdoor soccer, if a pass is a yard or two off the feet of the pass receiver and the opposing team is not playing closely, the pass receiver may be able to get the ball and keep going. In indoor soccer, a pass that is a yard or two off the foot of the receiver will likely never get to the receiver. Passes must be quick and accurate.

The same is true on the receiving end. A pass that is not forwarded with one touch must be trapped closely to avoid a bounce or roll out of the receiver's immediate control.

Passing into a space ahead of a running receiver is more difficult in indoor soccer as well. The timing of a pass must be just right to avoid overshooting and having the defense step up or having the opposing goal keeper come out and intercept the pass. Defensive players accustomed to clearing the ball upfield and having a quick forward chase the ball down will find that tactic does not work well inside. A long useless ball, or LUB, won't get the desired result, and it will be called back if it crosses three lines in the air.

Tactic: Attack with speed

Time always favors the defense. It allows defensive players to get back into their own zone and set up. It allows the defenders to determine whom they will cover in a man to man defense and communicate that among themselves.

Unless the offense is a man down on an attack, *it should always try to speed up the play to strike before the defense sets up.* At even strength or in a man (or two) advantage, the offense should continue moving downfield quickly and get a shot off as soon as possible. Recognize that while time favors the defense, speed favors the offense.

If the offense can take a shot on goal before the defense gets set, there is a possibility of a goal or a rebound shot. If the offense has pressed forward quickly, the players can get behind the defenders and get in position to make a rebound shot.

Keep in mind that the opponents will likely go to a man to man defense once the ball comes into their end. They will be marking the players as they come into the zone, and this can take some time to organize. This is another reason for the offense to speed up the play. See Exhibit 5-1 for an offensive push that should not slow down.

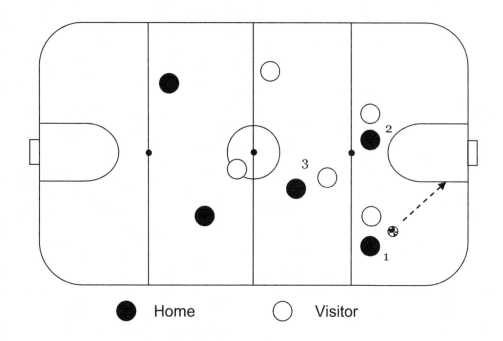

Home ●   Visitor ○

Exhibit 5-1

In this setup, it makes sense for Home player number 1 to shoot. He may score or Home player 2, who got inside Visitor player 2, can get the rebound. It does not make sense for Home player 1 to slow the play and wait for player 3. If he did that, the Visitor defense would drop back and have a better chance to defeat the play.

Tactic: Avoid getting stuck in corners

In Exhibit 5-1, Home player 1 gets a shot on goal. If he waits for player 3 and does not shoot, the Visitor defenseman will try to drive him to the corner as in Exhibit 5-2 below.

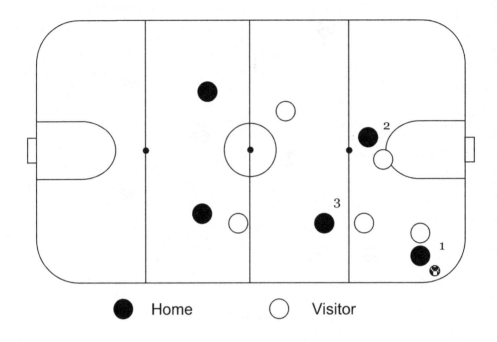

Home   Visitor

Exhibit 5-2

In this case, which occurs about 2 seconds after Exhibit 5-1 (without a shot), the defense has recovered and completely shut down the Home offensive push. Home player 1 waited for Home player 3, but got stuck in the corner while the defense covered both 2 and 3. Time favored the defense as the dribbler got stuck in the corner.

This scenario happens very frequently in indoor soccer. Many coaches in outdoor instruct their players to head for the corners and cross the ball in with a lofting cross. This works very well to draw the defense out of the goal area on a large field, but it does not work at all in an indoor arena.

Tactic: Get in position

In the event a forward does go deep into the corner and remains free, the other team members must get in position to take advantage of the situation. If only one other player has made it downfield in the fast break, that player must get in position to get a rebound shot as in Exhibit 5-3.

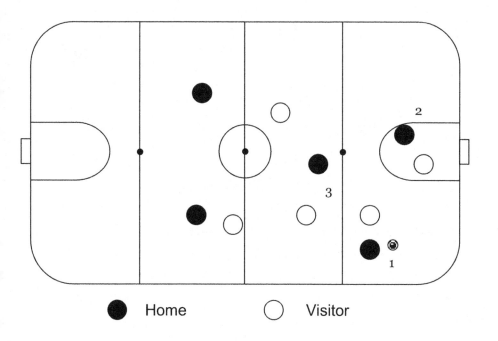

Exhibit 5-3

In this situation, Home player 2 is far enough out to get a rebound. As the play develops and Home player 2 sees Home player 3 coming downfield, player 2 can move forward as player 3 moves in to take his place as in Exhibit 5-4.

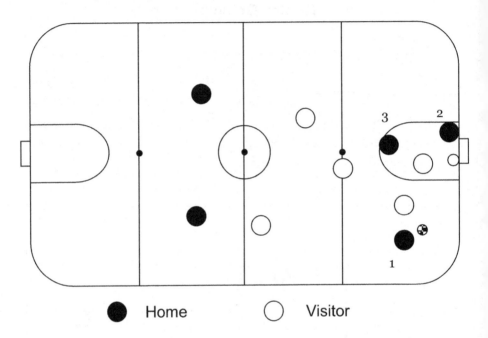

| ● Home | ○ Visitor |

Exhibit 5-4

Home player 2 is now on the far post to receive a pass. He is too far forward to receive a rebound, but player 3 is now in position to get the rebound. The keeper (shown as a smaller circle) will be covering the near post.

Notice that this is a low pressure strategy for the Home team. Notice also the large gap between

Home players 1, 2, and 3 and the other two Home defenders. Even though the Home team has a numerical superiority in this scenario, the Visitor team will have a 3 v 2 fast break in the event of a turnover. If teams commit to sending players deep into the opponents' end of the field, they need to ensure the players can get back out quickly.

Tactic: Keep moving

Sometimes it is difficult to create fast breaks. Some teams play with a very conservative low pressure system where defensive players stay back and the others can drop back quickly. If the opponent plays a 2-2-1 system (see Exhibit 4-2) it can be very difficult to get numerical superiority.

If the offense cannot get a fast break, the alternative is to bring the ball downfield with methodical passing and work for an opening to shoot. In this case, the game takes on a similarity to basketball where all ten players are in one end and the offense passes the ball around until it creates an opening.

In this situation, the offense must become fluid and keep moving. The concept of staying in position, which is so important in outdoor soccer, becomes less important than getting open for a pass, or "showing" for the ball. The forwards might cross left to right, the defenders may roll and switch with the forwards, and the midfielder(s) may charge the goal or attempt to screen the goal keeper.

A team may have pre-determined plays that are practiced ahead of time, as in basketball. Most of the time, however, the offense will play more like a hockey team looking for an open player or an opportunity to take a shot on goal. See Exhibit 5-5 for examples of staying fluid.

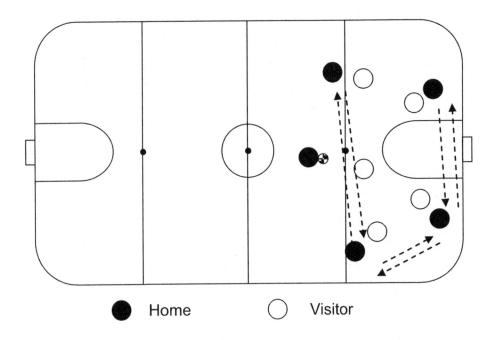

Home   ○ Visitor

Exhibit 5-5

This movement and changing of positions is sometimes difficult for players transitioning from

48

outdoor soccer to pick up. The concept of left/right and forward/back are less prescriptive in indoor than they are in outdoor soccer. Some coaches and teams at the recreational level do not differentiate between left and right. They have forwards, midfielders, and backs. Players need to be able to play left or right equally as well.

In this fluid movement, players cannot wait around for passes. The defense will challenge the ball carrier immediately in its own end, and the ball carrier must have options available immediately to avoid a turnover.

Tactic: Use the walls

Some players get used to the side walls pretty quickly. A rebound off the side wall is easy to use to get around an opponent if the opponent is not ready for it. The offensive player with the ball can either pass to a teammate downfield or run around the challenger and retrieve the rebound.

Side wall rebound passes are most common in the middle third of the field when a player is attempting a fast break and needs to get by one player to either make a pass to another player or get a clear run toward the opposing goal. The wall is used as if it were another player who is making a one touch pass.

Wall passes are less common in the attacking end because they often result in getting caught in a corner. However, they can be used in reverse if a player gets too deep and needs to back up.

Perhaps the most underutilized tactic in indoor soccer is the *intended* pass off the back wall. Most rebounds off the back wall are simply missed shots. When done properly, however, an intended pass off the back wall to another player is very difficult to defend against.

Consider the situation in Exhibit 5-6. The player with the ball has no clear shot on goal and is being forced into the corner. The Home teammate in the penalty area is covered, but is perfectly situated to shoot on a one touch shot off the back wall. The goal keeper is positioned on the near post, but has little chance to make the save if the ball comes off the rebound as shown.

It is important to point out here that this tactic is often overlooked and seldom done well, but it is one of the most effective ways to score.

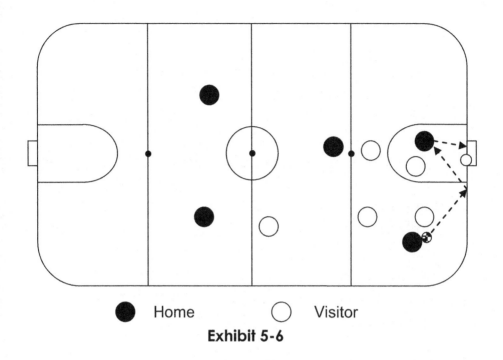

● Home   ○ Visitor

Exhibit 5-6

Tactic: Use one touch in close

Exhibit 5-6 demonstrates the need for one touch control skills in indoor soccer. The Home player in the penalty area must play the ball on the first touch. Otherwise the keeper and defenders will challenge immediately.

The ability to redirect the ball on the first touch is essential in indoor soccer. Just as in hockey, time does not allow the luxury of trapping, looking around, making a decision, and executing another pass or shot.

Attack Scenarios

An offensive attack can happen very quickly under a variety of circumstances. Indoor soccer is all about converting a transition, or turnover, into a scoring opportunity. When a breakaway occurs, there will typically be one, two, or three offensive players sprinting downfield against one, two, three, or four defensive players. We will cover the most common combinations in this section. The terminology used here will be in the format of X v X where the first number represents the number of offensive players attacking versus the number of defensive players in the play.

1 v 1

In a 1 v 1 scenario, it makes sense for the ball carrier to dribble and attempt to get by the defender. Here is what the ball carrier should do:

- If the defender backs up, the ball carrier should cut inside.
- If the defender charges, the ball carrier should shield and dribble, cut outside, or use a wall pass to get by the defender.
- If the ball carrier is quicker than the defender, the ball carrier can go around the outside of the defender and angle back toward the goal for a shot.

1 v 2

A 1 v 2 is not insurmountable. The player with the ball can do the following:

- If the defensive players are even with one another, the ball carrier can try to split the players down the middle and get a quick shot off.
- The ball carrier can make a wall pass off the back wall. The defense won't be expecting it and the offensive player will know where the ball is going. He or she might get a rebound shot by sprinting past the defenders who turn around to look where the ball went.
- The ball carrier can dump the ball into the corner and chase it. This turns a 1 v 2 into a 1 v 1 while creating enough time for another offensive player to enter the play, creating a 2 v 2. Warning: this also allows the defense time to get back.
- The ball carrier can stop at the red line and wait for help.

1 v 3

Some dribblers might welcome this scenario, but prudent players will wait for support.

2 v 1

If two offensive players are attacking with one defender:

- The offensive players should not get even with one another; they should strive to stagger. They should not let the defender get between them.
- The ball carrier should pass to the open player, if challenged, and prepare for a return pass or rebound shot off the back wall.
- If the ball carrier heads for the corner or gets driven to the corner, the other player should move to the top of the penalty area to prepare for a rebound off the back wall or pass across the middle. Support should be coming down the wall from the midfielder.
- If the defender covers the open player, ball carrier should shoot on goal.

2 v 2

The 2 v 2 scenario is quite common. There are a number of things the attacking team can do. The two attacking players can try to get the defense to inadvertently drop coverage on a player by using one of the following moves:

Cross and drop. Crossing is where the players cross paths and try to disrupt the defensive players so that they don't know which player to cover. In a cross and drop, the player with the ball crosses in front of her teammate and leaves the ball at her feet.

Cross and carry. This is the same as cross and drop, but the ball carrier keeps the ball. If the defense gets confused, one of the players may now be unguarded.

Cross and pass. This is similar to cross and carry, but the ball carrier immediately passes to her teammate who is showing for the ball.

Give and go. This is where one player passes to the other player, and she one touches it right back. This is typically used to get around a defensive player.

Stationary give and go. This is where the pass receiver is not moving and is facing the ball carrier as she approaches. The ball carrier passes to the stationary player who dumps it off to one side or the other for the original ball carrier to keep going. A variation on this is if the stationary player waits for the original ball carrier to run by and then does a heel pass to her after she runs past.

Dump-in pass. This is similar to a dump in pass in hockey where the ball carrier kicks the ball into a corner and the teammate runs after it. This pass has a low percentage of success, but can be useful in some circumstances, such as substitution.

In a 2 v 2 scenario, as in a 2 v 1, if the ball carrier heads for the corner, the other offensive player should go near the top of the penalty area to await a rebound or crossing pass. If this player goes too close to the goal, she will be out of the play if the ball comes off the back wall with a lot of speed.

2 v 3

In this case, the opposition has dropped back quickly to defend. The two offensive players can:

- Utilize one of the passing plays listed in the discussion of 2 v 2 passes above.
- Wait for a third offensive player to catch up. As always, this also allows the defense more time to drop back and set up. The 2 v 3 may turn into a 3 v 4 or a 3 v 5.

2 v 4

The offense has no downside to waiting for more offensive players to join the play.

3 v 1

Common sense says that this scenario should have a very high success rate for the offense. However, mistakes often cause the offense to lose an excellent scoring opportunity. In a 3 v 1, keep the following in mind:

- The offense should keep the speed of the play up. In a 3 v 1, some players have a tendency to slow down to make sure they don't make a mistake. Slowing down *is* a mistake, because it allows more time for other defenders to get back.
- The ball carrier should move away from the boards to the middle of the field while moving quickly toward the opposing goal.
- The ball carrier should not try to dribble through the defender.
- If the defender covers one of the two open players, the ball carrier should shoot on goal.
- The three players should come down the field staggered, not in a line.
- If the ball carrier is challenged, he should pass the ball to one of the other open players and ensure the pass is accurate. A sloppy pass that ends up deep in the corner will give the defense more time to get back. A pass that is too far forward will give the goal keeper an opportunity to step up and intercept. The pass should give the pass receiver the opportunity to

shoot almost immediately upon receiving the ball.

- When a shot is taken, the two players without the ball should prepare for a one touch volley of a potential rebound.
- Shots should be very precise. An inaccurate shot that is kicked too hard will bounce off the back wall and result in a 4 v 2 going the other way.

3 v 2

The tactics used in a 3 v 2 are almost the same as a 3 v 1 and the offense should keep the same points in mind as listed for a 3 v 1. The unmarked player should get into a position to shoot. The ball carrier should pass to the open player if challenged, and should shoot if not challenged.

Some teams like to break the play down into a 2 v 1 and a 1 v 1. The offensive player without the ball that is being marked can go wide and deep, pulling the defenseman out of the play, leaving the remaining players in a 2 v 1.

No matter who ends up shooting, the shooter should realize that, like in a 3 v 1, an inaccurate shot that is kicked too hard can result in an offensive advantage for the opposition going the other way.

3 v 3

The 3 v 3 is similar to the 2 v 2 and the tactics remain similar. It can also be thought of as a 2 v 2 along with a 1 v 1. The offense needs to keep moving to create openings and it needs to keep passing until a shot can be taken.

The offense should be aware that the defense will play tighter or more closely in an even numbered attack. Therefore, the offensive players should be ready to be challenged immediately upon receiving the ball.

For all types of attacks, offensive players should keep the following in mind:

- All players involved in the attack should be aware of the scenario they are in (e.g., a 2 v 1, 3 v 2, etc.) and plan accordingly.
- The offense should initiate its attack as early as possible, preferably in its own end or in the middle third of the field.
- If the offense is superior or even in number, it should maintain or increase the speed of the play.
- The offense should stagger the players in its attack and avoid coming down the field in a line, or "square" to one another.
- If the offense is outnumbered, it should consider slowing the play and waiting for help.

- If the defense has had time to get set, the offense must keep moving to show for the ball.

Shooting

We have seen that there are many differences between indoor soccer and outdoor soccer. There are even more differences regarding shooting, including speed and accuracy.

Speed

When outdoor players start playing indoor soccer, it is sometimes comparable to a tennis player playing racquetball for the first time. There is a tendency to think that because the ball won't go out of bounds, it means you can hit the ball harder. Likewise, soccer players coming inside often think they can kick the ball *harder*.

The biggest mistake shooters make in indoor soccer is trying to kick the ball too hard. There is nothing wrong with hard, accurate shots. But the downside to hard, *inaccurate* shots is that they travel back the other way harder and faster as well. This is particularly troublesome on smaller fields where a ball can easily end up in the opposite end after a very hard inaccurate shot.

Accuracy

Shooting accuracy is extremely important in indoor soccer. Many shots end up going wide or high and out of play. In outdoor soccer, there may be very few shots on goal, but in indoor there may be 50 or more shots on goal. In outdoor play, missed shots result in a goal kick which means the ball will go 60 yards back the other way.

What happens to the shots in indoor play? They do one of the following:

- Go in for a score
- Get collected by the goal keeper
- Go high and out of bounds
- Stay in play

It is this last point that makes all the difference. Missed shots stay in play and create turnovers or, if the offense is properly positioned, additional scoring opportunities.

The more accurate the shot, the better chance the offense has to make a follow up shot. If a shot misses by a few inches, a teammate can be in position to get the rebound. If it misses by several feet, the teammate has no idea where to be.

Shooting tactics

Here are a few things to remember about shooting:

- You can't shoot too low. You maintain better control and the keeper can only fall as fast as gravity will allow.
- Shoot fast for surprise. Avoid large windups and shoot quickly.
- Use toe kicks, heel kicks, outside of the foot kicks, and kicks with no windup to add to the element of surprise.
- Inside the penalty area, strive for one touch shots.
- On an initial shot, shoot across the mouth of the goal to the far side. Most goal keepers will hug the inside post, so always try to aim for the far post (see Exhibit 5-7).

In Exhibit 5-7, Home player number 1 is shooting at the far post (keeper shown on near post). If it is wide right, player 2 is in position to get the rebound. If the shot is short to the left, player 3 is ready for the rebound.

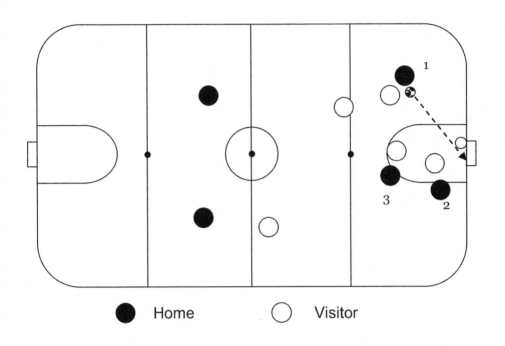

Home ●   **Visitor** ○

Exhibit 5-7

Chapter 6: Defense

Defense in indoor play is a game of constantly challenging for the ball. In our discussion of defense, we will cover defensive tactics followed by defensive scenarios.

Defensive Tactics

Tactic: Delay, delay, delay

As we saw in our study of offense, time favors the defense. Time allows defenders to get back into position and regain numerical parity or superiority. There are many ways to increase time for the defense, but the simplest ways are:

- Start the challenge in the neutral zone. If the defense can put up a challenge in the middle third of the field, it will give the other players time to get back.
- Drive the offense to the walls. If an offensive player is against the wall, he or she only has 50% of the amount of room to maneuver. Trapping a player against the wall buys time and gives teammates the opportunity to get back.
- Drive the offense deep into the corners. This gives the offensive player very few choices. If

the defense drives the ball carrier into the corner, the defense should cover the goal-side wall so that the ball carrier cannot dribble by or make a pass or shot along the back wall. (See Exhibit 6-1.)

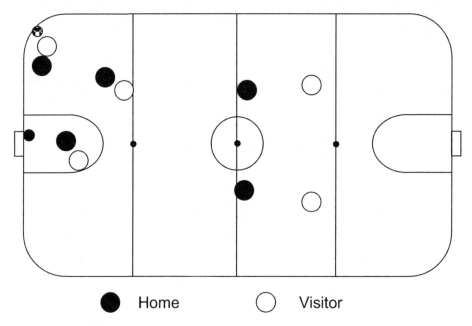

● Home   ○ Visitor

Exhibit 6-1

Exhibit 6-1 shows an effective move by the Home defender to drive the Visitor player into the corner while covering the goal-side wall. The other two defenders have come back to cover the remaining two Visitor forwards. The ball carrier has very few options.

Tactic: Go man to man

The defense should go man to man inside its own zone. This will be uncomfortable for outdoor players making the transition, but if attackers are left alone for only a few steps, they can be shooting on goal.

The defense can play a modified zone in the neutral zone. A modified zone means the defensive players will need to communicate their intentions to one another. If a defender lets an attacker go, he or she needs to tell the other defender to pick up the runner.

Tactic: Play close

Defensive players need to play closer to their opponents than their outdoor counterparts. Most players don't play close enough in indoor soccer.

Gap control, or managing the space between players, is crucial in indoor soccer. Playing too loosely results in too many shots on goal. Playing too closely, on the other hand, can result in the defenders over-committing.

Notice in Exhibit 6-1 that the Home defenders are playing very closely in their own end and the forwards are looser in the neutral zone.

Tactic: Challenge quickly

One of the toughest things players have to get used to in indoor soccer is how little time they have before they get challenged for the ball. This is mainly because the field is more compact and the players are closer together.

Defenders need to challenge for the ball almost all the time in their own zone because the offense can shoot from just about anywhere. Defenders can feint a challenge in the neutral zone to slow the attackers down, but the defenders need to be careful not to over-commit if they are the last defender to the goal.

One of the best ways to challenge without over-committing is to poke or stab at the ball. If a defender can get a toe on the ball to make it change direction, this is often enough to disrupt the entire play. In outdoor play where there is more room to play, this tactic may not have a great effect on the ball carrier, since he or she may be able to recover in a larger space. But in indoor soccer, other players are usually very close by and can help finish off the disruption of the play.

This is a very effective tactic, but it is vastly underutilized. Too many defenders allow the ball carrier to dribble down the field without challenging or trying to disrupt the play.

Occasionally a coach might yell, "Stick your foot out!" This means get a toe on it to make the ball carrier lose control. Two defenders, each getting a toe on the ball in succession, can frustrate the dribbler and cause a turnover.

Tactic: Don't let them shoot

This sounds straightforward, yet many teams don't challenge when an attacker is just outside the penalty area directly in front of the goal. Perhaps this is a carryover from outdoor soccer. While the penalty area is significantly smaller in indoor soccer than it is in outdoor soccer, the strength of the kickers' legs is the same. So just because someone is outside the penalty area in indoor soccer it does not mean that they are less of a threat if they shoot. Anyone inside the defense's red line is a threat, and some powerful shooters are a threat outside the line.

Defenders should challenge or screen the ball carrier from shooting at all times when the ball carrier is inside the defense's red line. A ball carrier with a fraction of a second can get a shot off with a clear line to the goal. To create as much of a problem as possible for the shooter, the defender should stay on line between the ball carrier and the center of the goal. See Exhibit 6-2.

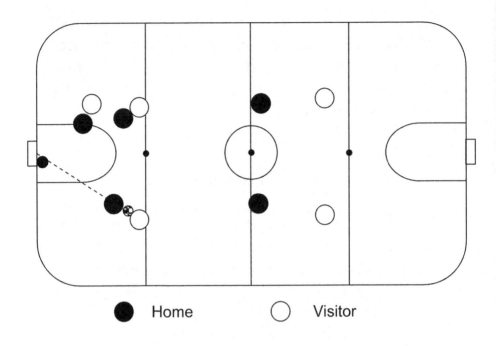

Home ●   **Visitor** ○

Exhibit 6-2

In Exhibit 6-2, if the ball carrier steps to his left or right, the defender must stay in front of the player in line with the goal at very close range to prevent the ball carrier from shooting. Notice that the other two defenders are playing very closely and are positioned to keep the attackers from receiving a pass.

It is important to remember that the defense needs to be playing man to man in this scenario. If the ball carrier starts to drag to his right toward the center of the field and the defender releases for another defender to pick up the ball carrier, it is a free shot for the offense.

Tactic: Don't stare at the ball

A common mistake of defenders is staring at the ball when the opponent with the ball is being covered by another defender. When defenders watch the ball instead of the opponent they are covering, that opponent will run away and get open. This happens very frequently in recreational play. Defenders should watch the player they are covering and glance at the ball to see where it is going.

Avoid LUBs

In the event the defense acquires the ball from the offense by challenging or by recovering a rebound, the defense should not kick a LUB, a long useless ball, downfield. A LUB is common in outdoor play at the recreation levels, and sending the ball 30 or 40 yards downfield can end an offensive push.

In indoor soccer, a LUB can momentarily relieve the defense of pressure, but it can be dangerous for two reasons:

1. It can result in a three line foul which will bring the ball back to the defensive red line and the offense will be awarded a free kick.
2. The LUB will be retrieved by the opponent's defenders and they can immediately renew

their attack. They can be shooting again with one accurate pass.

If the offense is pounding the goal with a series of shots and the defense has not been able to regain possession, a LUB may feel like a reprieve when the defense finally gets a foot on the ball. However, in most cases, the LUB provides only a short reprieve until the offense resets and begins again.

Whenever the defending team does get the ball, its midfielders and forwards should be ready immediately to sprint upfield to show for a transition pass.

Tactic: Don't dribble in your own zone

This is good advice for outdoor soccer, but it applies even more in indoor soccer. Look at Exhibit 6-2 again. If the Home team gets possession, it has two forwards open that are available to get a pass. With the exception of a high pressure situation, the defense will almost always have an open player to pass to upon taking possession in a turnover situation.

The downside for the defense dribbling in its own end is the possibility of losing the ball and having an immediate shot on its goal. Any shot taken inside the red line is a threat, even for younger players whose shots are not always strong.

Another less obvious reason for the Home team not to dribble in its own end is that it gives the Visitor team time to get back and set up. The Visitor player who lost possession in the Home end may stay and try to challenge. In this case, the longer the Visitor player challenges and keeps the Home player tied up, the more time the rest of Visitor team has to get back.

There are a few exceptions to this advice. For example, if the opposing team employs a high pressure strategy, there may be an opportunity for a player to dribble out of her own end if she takes possession and there are no opposing players in front of her. If she is quicker than the opposition's defenders, she may go the length of the field and get a shot off. However, this happens very rarely.

We will cover the transition game later in the book, but for the purposes of this section, teams should avoid dribbling in their own ends.

Defensive Scenarios

As a reminder, in the terminology of X v X presented here, the first number is the number of offensive players and the second number is the number of defensive players in the given scenario.

1 v 1

In a 1 v 1, the primary aim of the defender should be to keep the attacker from shooting. The defender should try to stand up to the offensive player as early as possible, preferably in the neutral zone. This will slow down the play and allow the other defenders time to get back.

When the attacker pushes forward, the defender should do the following:

- If the attacker is fast, the defender should back up and move toward the center of the field, forcing the attacker to the outside. At the top of the penalty area, the defender should stop backing up and challenge.
- If the defender can force the attacker to the outside and along the wall, the defender should keep the attacker pressed to the wall and down into the corner.
- If the attacker gets by, the defender should turn and stay with the attacker, remembering to try to touch the ball to disrupt the attacker ("Stick your foot out!")
- If the attacker passes to another player, the defender should *continue covering that player* and resist chasing the ball from player to player.

1 v 2

When one attacker comes at two defensive players, one defender should challenge the attacker as if it were a 1 v 1, and the other should wait for the next offensive player to join the play. The second defender should avoid double teaming the attacker so that a trailing offensive player does not come in uncovered. The defenders should stay staggered and avoid getting caught side by side so the attacker can't split them.

If the attacker takes a shot, the second defender should be ready for the rebound. If the keeper collects the ball, the second player should be ready to accept a pass from the keeper and prepare to transition to offense.

1 v 3

One attacker should not attack three defenders. If this happens, one of the defenders should take on the attacker and treat it as a 1 v 1, while the remaining defenders provide support and balance.

2 v 1

When a defender is facing two attackers, the defender should do the following:

- Get between the attackers in the neutral zone and delay the play as much as possible.
- Cover the attacker that is closer to the middle of the field as the play develops across the red line.
- If the goal keeper is strong, the defender should cover the player without the ball and let the keeper take the shooter. There are two exceptions to this:

  - If the shooter is known to be stronger than the non-shooter;
  - If the keeper wants the defender to take the ball carrier in a 2 v 1, the defender should do so.

- Listen to the keeper. The keeper can see the whole play developing. The keeper will ultimately have to defend the shot if one is taken, so the keeper should direct the defender as needed. If the keeper believes there is a better chance of the attacker making a poor pass than of making a good shot, the keeper should call the defender to cover the attacker with the ball. If the keeper has a preference, he or she should remind the defenders of that preference before each game.
- Prevent a rebound shot. The defender should be ready for the ball to come off the back wall and prepare for transition to offense.

2 v 2

A 2 v 2 is really two 1 v 1's. The more dangerous player is the attacker without the ball, so the defender covering that player needs to play very closely. The defenders should communicate and expect the passing plays we covered in the 2 v 2 discussion in chapter 5. The defenders should communicate and switch their coverages when necessary.

When a defender is covering an attacker with the ball in a 2 v 2 scenario, the defender should attempt to drive the attacker to the wall and then into the corner if possible. This will slow down the play and give a third defender time to get back. The second defender can expect his player without the ball to get in the penalty area to get a pass or rebound. The defender should position himself between the attacker and the goal so that the attacker cannot make a one touch shot if the ball comes to the attacker.

See Exhibit 6-3.

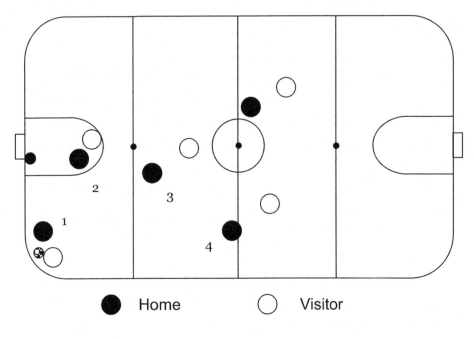

● Home   ○ Visitor

Exhibit 6-3

Exhibit 6-3 shows a 2 v 2 where Home defender 1 has driven the attacker into the corner and Home defender 2 is covering inside. Home midfielder 3 is ensuring a third attacker is covered and Home forward 4 is covering the wall.

2 v 3

When two attackers take on three defenders, the defenders should treat this as a 1 v 1 and a 1 v 1, with the third defender waiting for a third attacker to come down the field. The third defender should avoid double teaming the attacker with the ball in order to be ready for any other attackers coming or provide backup ("second defender") to the defender challenging the ball.

3 v 1

This is a tough situation. When three attackers get a breakaway on one defender, the defender should stay in the middle and listen to the keeper. The defender should challenge any attacker that gets in the penalty area. If the lone defender challenges, he should try to push the ball carrier towards the outside, but maintaining a position that inhibits a good pass to a player in a shooting position. The defender's positioning is critical in this situation.

3 v 2

In a situation where three attackers take on two defenders, the defense should treat this as a 2 v 1 and a 1 v 1. The defense should stand up to the offensive attack as early as possible, in the neutral zone if possible, and try to delay the play until the third defender can get back.

The defender covering the ball should get between the attacker with the ball and the goal and push the attacker to the outside if possible. The other defender should cover the attacker closer to the ball carrier to force the pass to the attacker that is further away. See Exhibit 6-4.

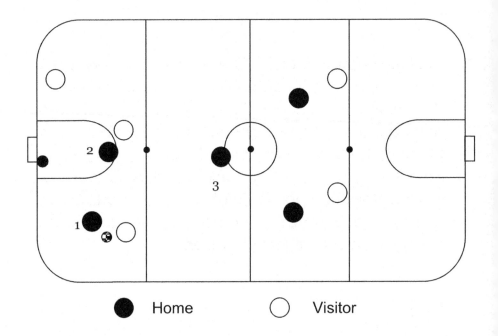

Exhibit 6-4

In Exhibit 6-4, Home defender 1 is pressing the ball carrier to the corner. Home defender 2 is covering the near attacker. If the attacker with the ball tries to make a pass to the open attacker near the goal, the ball has a longer distance to travel and can be intercepted by Home defender 2 or the keeper. Defender 3 should hurry back and cover.

3 v 3

A 3 v 3 matchup is quite common. The defense needs to stay man to man and exercise great care if the offensive players without the ball keep moving around. Their purpose, of course, is to keep moving to get passes and keep looking for an opportunity to shoot.

The defense should play very close (goal side) to the players they are covering. The defender covering the player with the ball should challenge inside the red line while being careful not to over-commit. The defender must keep challenging, particularly in the penalty area. By allowing even one step of freedom on the ball carrier, the defender is allowing a potential shot on goal. Finally, the defenders covering the players without the ball must not be tempted to leave the attackers they are covering to help the defender challenging the ball, unless it is clear that double teaming the ball carrier will result in a turnover.

For all types of defensive scenarios, defensive players should keep the following in mind:

- All players involved in the attack should be aware of the scenario they are in (e.g., 2 v 1, 3 v 2, etc.) and plan accordingly.

- The defense should stand up to the attack as early as possible, preferably in the middle third of the field.
- If the offense is superior or even in number, the defense should slow the play down as much as possible. Time helps the defense to get set and gather additional help.
- If the defense is outnumbered, it is almost always best for a defender to push the ball handler outside. It is easier for a goal keeper to defend a shot from the ball carrier because he can be in the proper position. It is harder for a keeper to defend a quick 'one touch' shot off a well placed pass because the keeper will be out of position or in motion trying to get into position.
- When even or superior in number, the defense should play man to man in its own zone and stay very close to the attackers.
- Defenders should not stare at the ball; they should cover their players and glance at the ball.

Chapter 7: The Transition Game

The transition game is one of the most important dynamics in indoor soccer. *Dynamic* transitions, or turnovers, can happen anywhere on the field. They can happen in:

- A team's own zone upon keeper acquisition of the ball
- A team's own zone when the defense successfully challenges for the ball
- A team's own end on a rebound
- The neutral zone
- The opponent's end on a rebound
- The opponent's zone by its defense
- The opponent's zone by its keeper

Static transitions, by contrast, are when the ball changes possession at a stop in play, such as:

- Out of bounds balls resulting in goal kicks, corner kicks, or kicks from the touch lines (side lines) where the ball left the field
- After a scored goal
- After a penalty

We will cover static turnovers with set plays and special plays in Chapter 10.

How Transitions Occur

There are three times when a dynamic transition can occur. They happen after:

1. The keeper takes possession of the ball
2. A dribbler is successfully challenged
3. A pass is not completed

It is this third item, the incomplete pass, that accounts for most turnovers. Incomplete passes come in the form of inaccurate passes, passes that are too slow, passes that are bobbled by the receiver, intercepted passes, and LUBs out of the defensive area.

As we discussed in Chapter 3, passing is extremely important in indoor soccer. Teams that can pass well can literally run their opponents around in circles. The most effective way for an offense to reduce turnovers is to continue to practice accurate passing. The most effective way for a defense to increase turnovers is to stay close to the offensive players and challenge them as early as possible to force an incomplete or inaccurate pass.

This advice may sound simplistic, but the fundamental skill of challenging passes and forcing turnovers is often the biggest difference between great teams and not so great teams in indoor soccer.

What to do: defense to offense

Upon a turnover, the offense must immediately assess the scenario to determine the nature of the attack. For example, the players must understand if the attack is a 2 v 2, 3 v 1, etc. The offense should speed up the play and begin sprinting toward the opponent's end of the field. All too often, teams will take possession, stop, look around, and assess the situation. When this happens, the defense is resetting and the offense is losing its advantage.

If the ball is taken in a team's own defensive zone, the player with the ball should first look to see if there is a teammate sprinting downfield for a breakaway pass. That sprinting player should be showing for a pass in a manner that does not require the ball carrier to pass up the middle of the field or cross the field with a long pass.

In Exhibit 7-1, Home player should pass to Home player 4 with a wall pass rather than pass to player 3 even though player 3 appears more open. A pass to player 3 has a high chance of being intercepted. Once Home player 4 gets the ball, she is in a 3 v 2 with teammates 3 and 5.

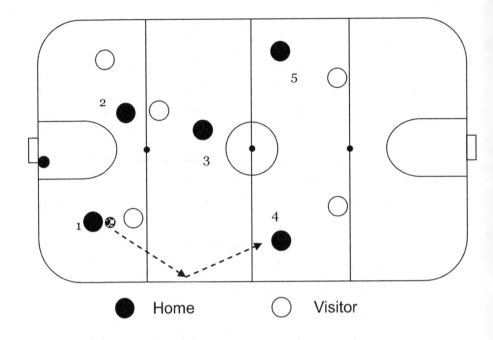

Exhibit 7-1

The best time to use the walls is in transition play moving into or out of the neutral zone. Side wall passes are not as effective deep in a defensive zone because the angle of the deflection is too high. When the angle is high, it is easier for the opposing team to intercept. See Exhibit 7-2.

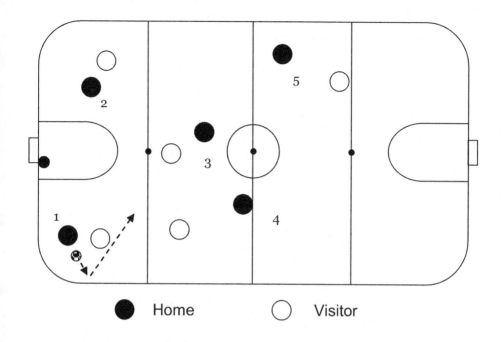

Exhibit 7-2

In Exhibit 7-2, Home player 1 should NOT make the wall pass as shown. It will almost certainly be intercepted. Home player 1 should shield (clockwise as shown) and pass back to the keeper.

The walls can be a great asset and can often be used very creatively. However, using the side wall is not always the best choice. This is particularly true if an offensive player gets stuck in a corner. If the ball is too deep in the offensive zone, a kick off the sidewall is easier to defend than a back wall pass or a direct pass. See Exhibit 7-3.

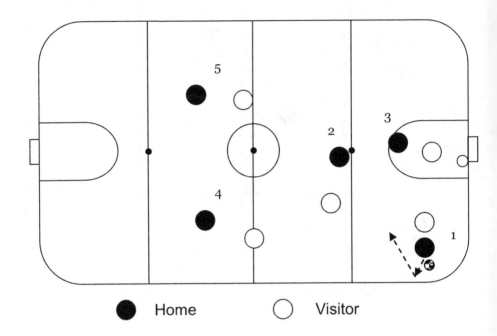

Exhibit 7-3

Home player 1 in Exhibit 7-3 would be better off making a back wall pass to Home player 2 or 3 than making the side wall pass shown.

Compare Exhibits 7-2 and 7-3 to Exhibit 7-1. Notice that the play will accelerate in 7-1 on the transition, while it will likely slow down in 7-2 and 7-3. Remember, the key to transitioning to offense is to speed up and try to get the numerical advantage.

What to do: offense to defense

After losing possession of the ball, the first thing a player should do is try to win the ball back. In many cases, players lose a ball and immediately transition to defense. Trying to win the ball back has two purposes: to get the ball back and to slow down the counter attack.

If a team loses the ball, it should first try to stand up to the opponent as soon as possible whether it is in its own zone, the neutral zone, or the opponent's end. The team that lost the ball should immediately assess the situation and determine if the opponent will have a numerical advantage.

The defending team can go into a zone defense in the neutral zone, but must go to a man to man defense once the ball comes into its own zone. It is a very dangerous time when the ball is coming into the defender's zone. This is the time when the defenders should be identifying the players they will be covering, and the players need to communicate to one another about their intentions.

Unfortunately, some teams break down here. Sometimes midfielders don't transition completely to defense, and they sometimes tend to let the player they were covering slide across the red line with the hope a defender will pick him up. If the two defenders already have two attackers to cover, this will create a man advantage for the offense. This is another instance where it sounds like this would be a rare occurrence, but it happens quite frequently. Perhaps this is a vestige from outdoor thinking where midfielders or forwards are not used to coming all the way back to defend. See Exhibit 7-4.

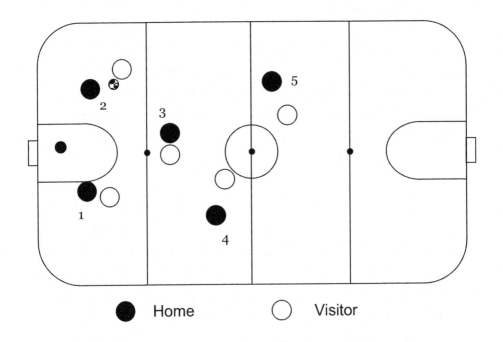

Exhibit 7-4

In Exhibit 7-4, Home player 3, a midfielder, must stay with his player, even if that player goes all the way to the goal or to the corners. Player 3 must become a full defender to prevent a 3 v 2 advantage for the Visitor team.

Once the transition has occurred, the defending team should play according to the particular defensive scenarios discussed in Chapter 6.

Chapter 8: Substitution

Substitution is "on the fly" in indoor soccer, meaning that it can happen at any time. Substitution is also unlimited, so the players can come in and out as much as the team desires.

Some teams play with line substitution, which means that the same players stay together. For example, a team may have two or more offensive lines and two or more defensive lines. If a line stays together, the players get to know how their teammates will play in certain situations.

In recreational play, line substitution may be less common than individual substitution. Substitutions sometimes happen at predetermined time intervals, but in many cases, players play until they are tired and then come out. A typical shift for a recreational level player is between four and five minutes.

Even though players may substitute individually, teams need to be aware of the talent mix on the field at any given time. Also, the players that are going in must be ready. For example, sometimes the players on the bench are watching the game intently at one end and do not notice a player coming off the field from the other end.

Substitutions generally occur just after change of possession, during transitions, or at stoppages in play. At the transitions, some teams substitute only when they have possession of the ball.

Other teams substitute lines or individuals when the ball is at the opposite end of the field from where the substituted players are coming out. For example, the defense might change when the ball is in the opponent's end and the offense might change when the ball is in their own end. This is the most common way of substituting if a team plays a low pressure strategy. See Exhibit 8-1.

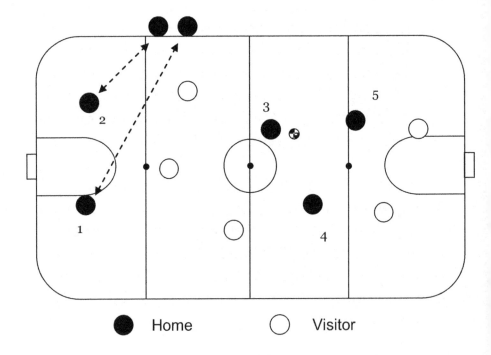

Exhibit 8-1

In Exhibit 8-1, Home players 1 and 2 substitute while Home players 3, 4, and 5 move toward the opponent's end.

Occasionally a team will dump a ball in, as in hockey. This means a team will kick a ball deep into the opponent's corner and substitute as the opponents chase the ball down. While this is popular in hockey, it is not as effective in indoor soccer. It creates a self-inflicted automatic turnover. It is better to pass the ball around and slow the play down, if possible, if the team desires a pre-planned substitution.

The biggest mistake a team can make in substituting is leaving the opposing team an opportunity to attack with a numerical advantage on a breakaway. Teams must be careful to substitute only when they know that scenario is highly unlikely. This is another thing that sounds very obvious, but it happens all the time in the field.

The key to all substitution is to get it done as quickly as possible. The players coming out must sprint to the bench. The rules at some facilities dictate that the player coming out must reach the touch line, or side line, before the player going in can go on to the field. Other facilities say a player can come onto the field but cannot have any influence on the play until the exiting player is completely off. Either way, the game is so fast and dynamic that the substitutions need to be quick and seamless.

Chapter 9: Goal keeping

The goal keeper is a special player in any sport, and the keeper in indoor soccer is no exception. The keeper must be very confident and must remain calm under the most exceptional circumstances. Remember, a keeper may sometimes face dozens of shots in a game, many of which will get by. The keeper must be able to shake off any discouragement and get ready for the next play.

There are some significant differences between goal keeping in outdoor soccer and indoor. They are:

- *There are rebounds.* The shots that miss by a foot or two to either side of the goal are very difficult to handle. They may be just out of reach for the keeper, but if the shot was short to the near side, the ball comes off the wall directly in front of the goal. Shots rebounding off the back wall can also hit the keeper and then bounce into the goal.
- *The shots are closer.* Most of the shots on goal in indoor are at close range. Even the corner kicks are just a few feet away on smaller fields.
- *There are more shots.* A keeper may see a flurry of a half a dozen or more shots if the offense keeps possession. In an outdoor game, the keeper may have to jump up and down to

keep warm if he or she doesn't see a shot for 30 minutes on a cold day.

- *The keeper is more involved in the game.* Each time the keeper takes control of the ball, it is a transition play. The keeper may be responsible for 20 or 30 transitions per game. These transitions are different than an outdoor keeper punting the ball 60 yards downfield.
- *The keeper will block and deflect more.* Blocking and deflecting are great outdoor skills, but they are even more important in indoor soccer. With so many shots, the keeper must use any method available to protect the goal. This will mean more deflections.
- *The keeper will throw more.* Throwing the ball is extremely important in indoor soccer. A keeper throws or rolls the ball almost every time he touches it. A keeper who can't throw the ball properly or effectively is a HUGE liability,

Some goal keeping skills are the same for indoor as they are for outdoor. This section is not intended to cover all aspects of general goal keeping. There are other books that cover this in great detail. The following are tactics for goal keepers to keep in mind when playing indoors.

Tactic: Remember that everyone shoots

The goal keeper must be ready at all times because everyone shoots in indoor soccer. Occasionally a player will take a shot on goal from a kickoff. If a defender is blocking the view of the keeper or if the keeper is inattentive, a shot from a kickoff can result in a goal.

Shots will come from any part of the defensive half of the field. The addition of the three point line in some locations may increase the number of long distance shots. While the keeper has more time to react to a longer distance shot than a short one, a long shot can result in a deflection off of another offensive player or off of a defender, making a stop much more difficult. A long shot can also result in a rebound directly in front of the goal where a short range, one touch follow up shot can be very difficult to stop.

The lesson here is for the keeper to be ready at all times.

Tactic: Protect the near post

The keeper should protect the near post to prevent the easy shot from slipping in when shots are taken from one side or the other. By blocking the near post, the shooter is forced to aim across the goal which will result in a much higher angle shot. Shots that are directed to the far side will go wide if they miss and will not end up right back in front of the goal. See Exhibit 9-1.

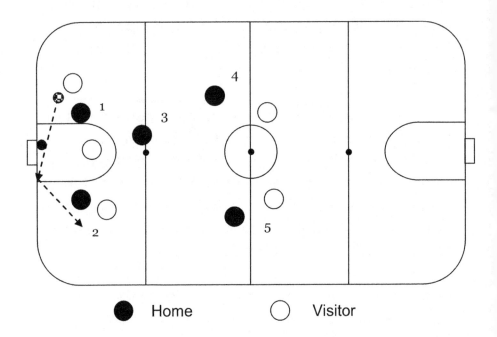

Exhibit 9-1

In Exhibit 9-1, the keeper forces the shot to the far side by covering the near post. The rebound goes to the far wall.

Another reason for covering the near post is that it is easier for the keeper to stop or deflect a shot that is short. This is a more dangerous situation than a shot that is long, because the rebound puts the ball in play directly in front of the goal. With one step up, the keeper can deflect or stop the ball from ending up in play in the penalty area. See Exhibit 9-2.

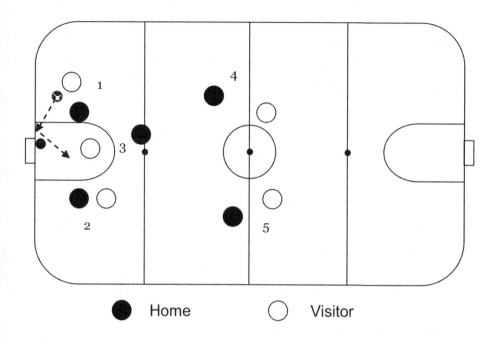

| ● Home | ○ Visitor |

Exhibit 9-2

In Exhibit 9-2, the keeper can step up and stop or block the shot, either before or after the rebound. Stopping this shot will keep this from becoming a very dangerous situation with two Visitor players in shooting position.

A final reason for hugging the near post is that by getting away from it, the keeper will have to dive or rush back toward it if the shot is between the keeper and the near post. These shots are dangerous to defend because the keeper can smash into the post or wall trying to get back. Some keepers learn to hug the near post *after* a hard crash.

The keeper and defense should be aware that most goals are scored across the mouth of the goal or on rebounds due to this goal keeping strategy.

Tactic: Come off the line

The keeper is very dynamic in indoor soccer. In most cases, the keeper should play at the top of the penalty area if the ball is at the opponent's end of the field. By staying at the top of the penalty area, the keeper can intercept balls breaking through the defense earlier than if he or she stays on the goal line. There is very little lead space in front of an offensive player on a breakaway, so if the keeper can step up, he can often disrupt the attack.

The keeper comes out of the penalty area and plays the ball with his feet much more in indoor than in outdoor soccer, and it requires more skill than just blasting a LUB. The main thing about being effective in this scenario is maintaining control. The keeper should just kick the ball gently to one side or against the side wall (preferably to a teammate) instead of kicking it hard out of bounds or into the roof. Keepers rarely dribble.

If a single opponent gets by the last defender and is now in a 1 v 0 against the keeper, the keeper should come off the line to narrow the angle on the attacker. The goal is smaller than in outdoor, so this tactic narrows the angle more in indoor than it does in outdoor. If the attacker gets inside the penalty area, the keeper can slide into the space in front of the feet of the attacker (if allowed by local rules) to disrupt the attack.

Tactic: Be vocal

The keeper must be very vocal in indoor soccer. Some keepers are quiet, but the best keepers are not shy about using their voices. The keeper can see the entire play and should tell the defense where to go. On free kicks, the keeper must keep the ball in sight at all times and the keeper must tell the players how to set up.

The keeper should also direct the players in the setup of a wall. The keeper must take command of the defense quickly and with authority. When using a defensive wall for an opponent's free kick, the defense should have no more than two players in the wall because more than two players in a wall will leave too many attackers undefended. The keeper should direct the free defenders to cover the open or moving attackers as the free kick is taken.

On free kicks on penalty spot some keepers have the two-man wall line up to left (or right) of center, forcing the shoot to go to the right (or left). The keeper stands just to the right (or left) of the wall, with a clear view of the ball. Having the wall in the center screens the keeper, and a good shooter can hit either corner.

Tactic: Study the opponents' shots

In outdoor soccer, a keeper may only get a shot or two from each of the different attackers. In indoor soccer, everyone shoots, and they often take multiple shots. Therefore, the keeper has the opportunity to get to know the shooting styles of the opponents relatively quickly.

For example, if an opponent has a forward that takes multiple shots on goal and all the shots go left, the keeper can begin to get an idea on how to defend that shooter. Some attackers shoot weakly, some shoot high, some take longer to shoot, some always push right before a shot, etc. The keeper can quickly assess the shooting tendencies of the attackers to build a distinct advantage.

Good shooters will shoot low. They will shoot low because shooting higher increases the chance of the ball going *too* high. The goal in most indoor facilities is 6' 6" high while it is 8' 0" high in outdoor soccer, so it is a little easier to extend upward in indoor play, if necessary. So if the keeper has no idea how an attacker will shoot, the keeper should stay low. Remember, the keeper can get down only as fast as gravity will allow.

Tactic: Transition to offense

Once the keeper takes possession of the ball, the team is on *offense*. Not understanding this concept is one of the biggest mistakes a team can make. Many teams stay in a defensive mode after the keeper has gained possession. If an opposing team picks up on this weakness early, it will pressure the keeper and defenders deep in their own zone after the transition.

In most cases, the distribution should be made very quickly. This gives the team the advantage of being in a potential breakaway situation. Some opposing forwards may not transition to defense immediately. The keeper and defense should take advantage of this by transitioning to offense as quickly as possible.

Once the keeper acquires the ball, he or she has five seconds (or sometimes eight, depending on local rules) to distribute it. Distribution is almost always with a throw or roll, but can sometimes be a ground pass. Young players can punt the ball, but if older players punt the ball they will almost certainly punt the ball across three lines. This brings the ball back to the defense's red line for a free kick for the opponents.

The distribution is crucial in indoor play. The keeper's teammates should give the keeper several choices to distribute the ball. See Exhibit 9-3.

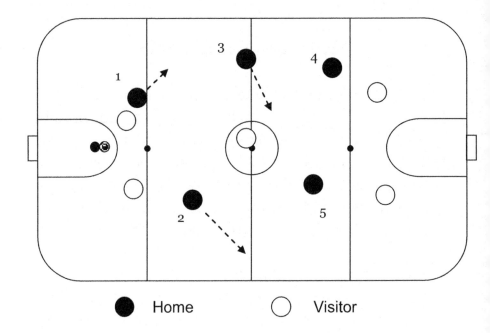

| ● Home | ○ Visitor |

Exhibit 9-3

In Exhibit 9-3, the keeper has just retrieved the ball and has run up to the top of the penalty area. The attackers have not yet retreated, so the keeper needs to make a quick release. Home player 1 is the short play, Home player 2 is the mid range play, and Home player 3 is the long play. *It is very important that the keeper feed the ball to the outside of player 1 or 2. If the keeper plays the ball to the inside of either one of them, the ball could be intercepted* and the attacker will go straight for the goal. This is a very common mistake.

Another common mistake is shown in Exhibit 9-4. It is outdoor mentality.

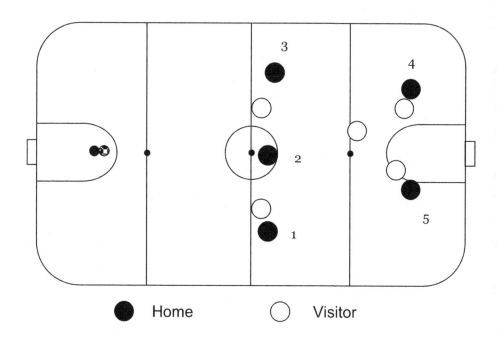

Exhibit 9-4

In Exhibit 9-4, the keeper waited until everyone reset. Home players 1, 2, and 3 all went to midfield to wait for the distribution and they are just standing there. If the keeper throws the ball, the Visitor players will very likely intercept and attack immediately. Even if Home players 1 and 3 cross and switch positions, all the Visitor forwards need to do is stand there and wait for the keeper to release and they will be in a very good position to intercept.

In the event the keeper is faced with the scenario shown in Exhibit 9-4, the keeper should throw the ball high to the outside of player 1 or 3, beyond the midfield line, so that it bounces off the wall.

In order to prevent the scenario in 9-4 from happening, the Home team should show a variety of options for the keeper.

Note: When distributing, a keeper should throw the ball very hard. Slow passes are almost always intercepted by a quick, aggressive player (again, due to the small field and close proximity). The keeper should lead his players, or throw it hard directly at their feet so they have a good chance to settle it quickly. Bouncing it to their chest is never a good idea.

In summary, the goal keeper is a much bigger part of the game in indoor soccer than in outdoor. He or she is involved in more plays, and plays a bigger role in those plays. The keeper must make more conscious decisions in the transition and distribution of the ball rather than just punting it 60 yards downfield.

Chapter 10: Set Plays and Special Plays

This chapter covers set plays and special plays. Set plays are plays from a dead ball such as kickoffs, kick-ins (from out of bounds), free kicks, corner kicks, and goal kicks. Special plays are power plays where one team is playing one or more players short due to penalties.

Set Plays

Set plays can provide a significant advantage for the kicking team. Many goals are scored on free kicks and corner kicks. Quite often, the best kicks are the ones that are taken before the defense has time to set up. Many facilities don't require the kicking team to wait for a second whistle to resume play. The play can start as soon as the ball is set, so the kicking can team take the kick almost immediately. In this case, simple is better: pass to an open player or take a shot.

If the defense gets set and puts up a wall or covers the kicking teams players, those players must move around and show for a pass. Sometimes, the kicker may decide to shoot while her teammates are moving around. Occasionally, one of the players can screen or shield the keeper momentarily so the kicker can get a clear shot. Set plays are also a great opportunity to *plan* a pass off of the back wall.

When defending a set play in their own zone, the defense should get set as quickly as possible to take away the quick kick opportunity. The defenders must play the opposition man to man and allow them as little space as possible. Defenders should also be aware of back wall passes and rebounds. If the defense sets a wall, the keeper should call it and direct it. The keeper must be able to see the ball at all times. See Exhibit 11-12 in Chapter 11 for a typical red line free kick set up.

Special Plays

Special plays, or power plays, are similar to those in hockey, but are less common. This is probably because many power plays in hockey are a result of penalties having to do with the stick, such as high sticking, hooking, tripping, obstruction, and other stick related penalties. While there may be five to ten penalties per team per game in hockey, there may be very few or none per team in an indoor soccer game. Penalties do occur, though, and they create a different dynamic in the game.

When a team has a man advantage in a power play, in most cases it will want to convert to a high pressure strategy if it is not already playing that way. This means the defenders will come up to assist the team with achieving the numerical advantage in the opposition's zone.

Many recreational teams do not have special positions predetermined for power plays. Just getting a man advantage is often all they may be concerned about. In these cases, the team with the advantage should do the following:

- Increase the speed of play
- Make quick, accurate passes
- Always look for the unmarked player

For teams that have specific power play formations, there are two main approaches.

The first formation is shown in Exhibit 10-1. It uses a single point player.

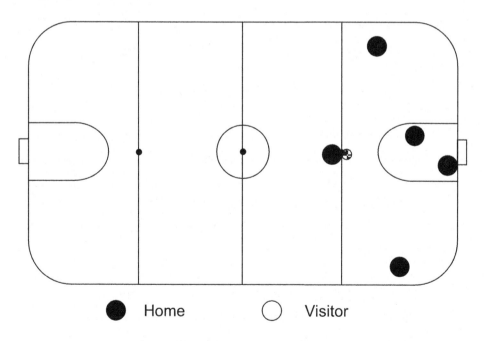

Exhibit 10-1

The other main approach uses two point players as shown in Exhibit 10-2. All other setups are variations on these two approaches.

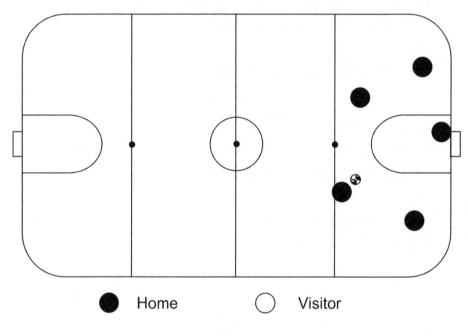

● Home   ○ Visitor

Exhibit 10-2

When employing one of the power play approaches, the offense must take care not to allow a breakaway by the other team. As in a normal high pressure strategy, the possibility always exists that one or two quick forwards on the opposing team can go the length of the field and score.

When a team is a man down, there are also two main formations. The more popular is a box formation shown in Exhibit 10-3. The diamond formation is shown in Exhibit 10-4.

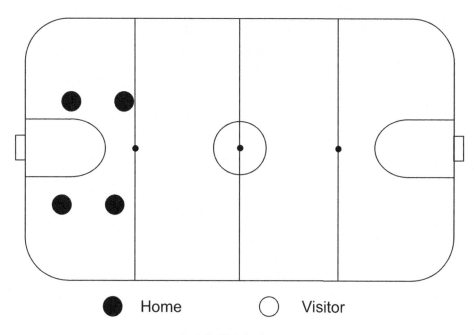

Exhibit 10-3

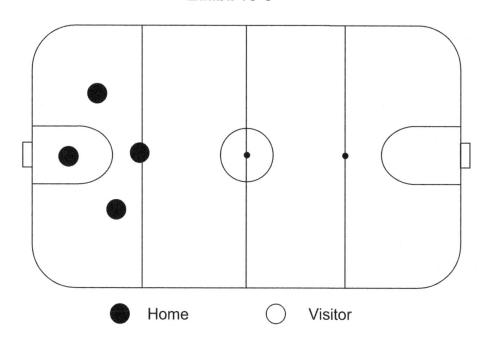

Exhibit 10-4

113

Either one of these formations will work and will depend on the individual strengths of the players and of the tactics of the opponents.

Chapter 11: Drills for Indoor Soccer

There are many books that show drills for basic soccer skills of dribbling, passing, and shooting. In those books, there are literally hundreds of drills that individuals or teams can do to improve in the basic skill areas. Please refer to those books to learn about them. This section will deal with drills specific to indoor soccer.

One of the challenges of practicing indoor soccer is getting field time. The managers of indoor facilities typically want to maximize the use of the fields for games, so indoor practices are not as common as outdoor practices. If a team does get indoor field time to practice, it will want to perform drills it cannot do outside.

The drills that follow are the core drills, or the basic drills, of indoor soccer and there are many variations of each.

Dribbling

Any drill where the player must play off the wall will increase his or her indoor playing skills. The following drill is very useful for getting players comfortable with what the ball will do in all areas of the field. The following drill can be set up on both sides of the field to maximize the space.

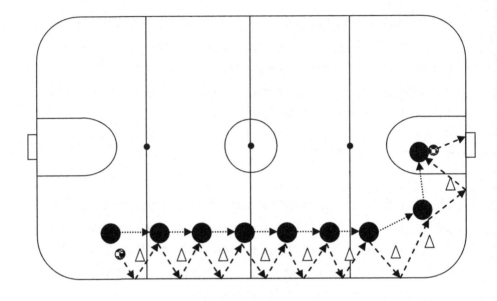

Exhibit 11-1

In Exhibit 11-1, the dribbler bounces the ball off the wall around the cones and keeps going until shooting.

Variations:

- Move the cones further from the wall.
- Change direction to practice with both feet.
- Eliminate some cones and have the dribbler move at different speeds.

Passing

Wall passes are an important part of indoor soccer. Most players transitioning to indoor play will try to use the walls, but the initial passes will be inaccurate. Practicing wall passes from all angles will improve this skill dramatically.

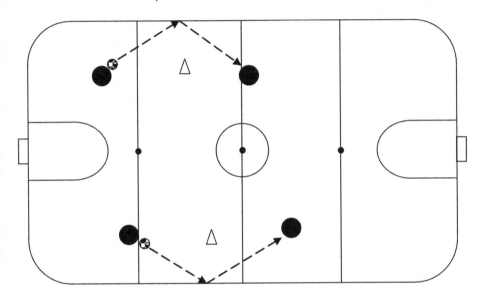

Exhibit 11-2

In Exhibit 11-2, players are practicing wall passes on each side of the field.

Variations:

- Have players kick the ball back and forth to each other.

- Players pass the ball to a third player (not shown) who shoots.
- Pass receiver turns and dribbles to the goal and shoots.
- Move the cones around the field so the players get a feel for passing in all locations.

Shooting

Teams that can shoot off the walls have a distinct advantage over those that are not as adept at this skill. The best drill for this is to have shooters in the penalty area and practice shots coming off the back wall as shown in Exhibit 11-3.

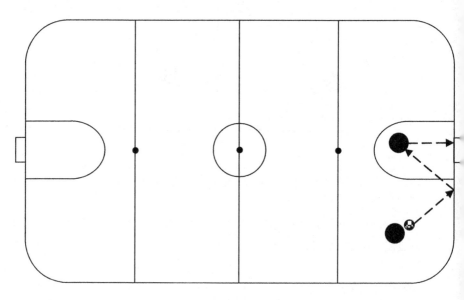

Exhibit 11-3

The drill shown in Exhibit 11-3 cannot be over-practiced. The drill must be performed over and over until the rebound is instinctive. When the players are in the opponent's penalty area, the ball can come at any speed and at any height, and the shooter must be able to handle it.

Variations:

- Move the passer around so that the pass comes off the back wall at different angles.
- Switch sides.
- Require that the shooter has only one touch.
- Make the receiving player start behind the red line and charge in.
- Add one or two defenders to the drill to make it closer to game conditions.

Sometimes shots are long and will rebound off the wall on the far side of the goal. In these cases, a player may have to serve the ball back into the penalty area for a shot, as in Exhibit 11-4.

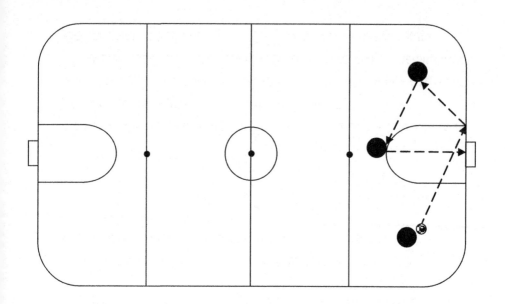

Exhibit 11-4

In Exhibit 11-5, the rebound shot is off the side wall.

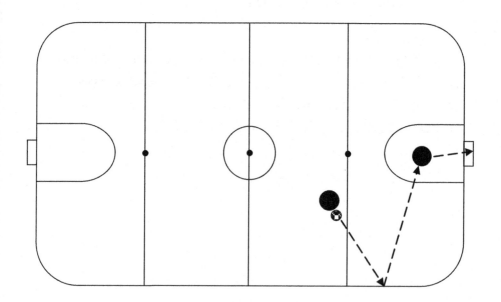

Exhibit 11-5

Variations:

- Switch sides.
- Alter angles.
- Add defenders.

Shooting at speed is an essential skill in indoor soccer. Many game scenarios result in a player breaking across the opponent's red line with one touch for a shot. In Exhibit 11-6, player 2 receives the pass from player 1 and accelerates to full speed with one touch to shoot on goal. Whether the drill is done with one touch plus a shot, or with one touch only, the shooter should be at top speed.

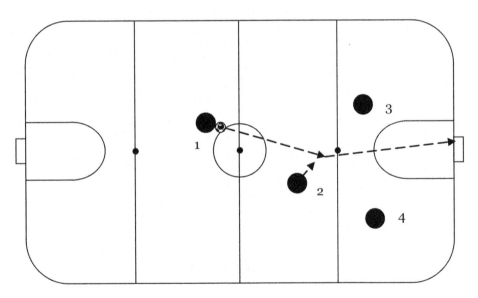

Exhibit 11-6

Variations:

- Make the pass come off the wall.
- Add a keeper to make the shot much more difficult.
- Have shooter two pass off the back wall and have players 3 and 4 shoot on rebounds.
- Add defenders to any of these variations.

Man-advantage scenarios

There are two types of man-advantage drills: *dynamic* and *static*. In the *dynamic* drill, the offense starts at its own end and presses downfield as if it is in a fast break. A 3 v 2 dynamic drill is shown in Exhibit 11-7:

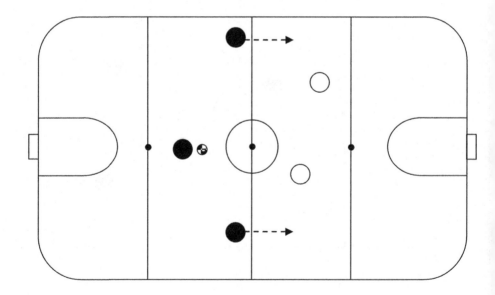

Exhibit 11-7

Variations:

- Have the Home keeper start with the ball and deliver it to the attackers so that they have to retrieve it on the run.
- Have the keeper deliver the ball to a different attacker each time.
- Adjust the scenario to a 3 v 1, 2 v 1, 4 v 2, etc.

A 2 v 1 scenario follows in Exhibit 11-8. This is a very common scenario, and the defense should have a standard operating procedure for this set up.

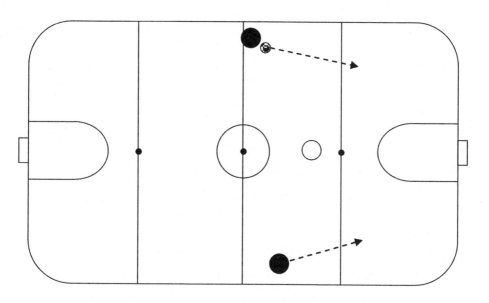

Exhibit 11-8

In a *static* drill, the offense starts at the attacking end of the field, as in Exhibit 11-9. A 3 v 2 is shown here.

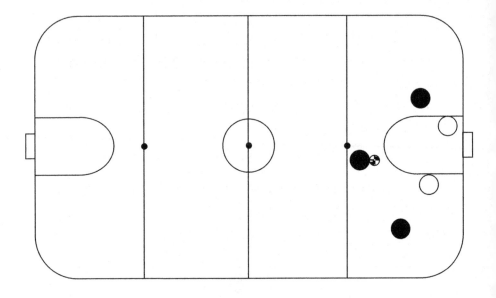

Exhibit 11-9

Variations:

- Adjust to 3 v 1, 2 v 1, 4 v 2, etc.
- Start the plays with wall passes.
- Add a goal keeper.

In all of the man-advantage scenarios, the team should reference chapters 5 and 6 of this book to determine the best ways to handle the scenarios.

Goal Keeping

The goal keeper will benefit from participating in all of the drills presented so far in this chapter. However, there are some drills that are particularly important for the indoor keeper to practice.

The first is the rebound off the back wall. This is the hardest thing for any keeper to cover well. The drill shown in 11-10 is similar to the shooting drill in Exhibit 11-3 with the keeper at the near post. In Exhibit 11-11, the keeper is allowed to stop the ball before it hits the back wall or just after it comes off the back wall.

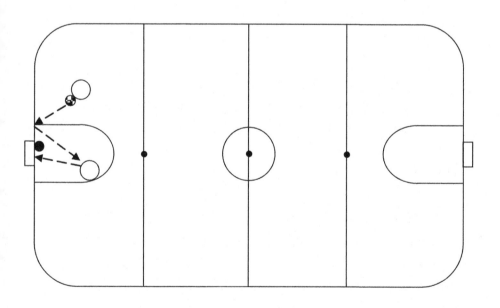

Exhibit 11-10

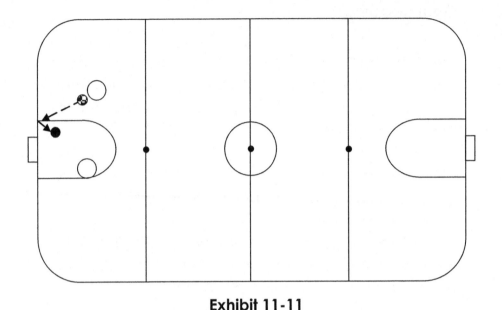

Exhibit 11-11

Variations:

- Move the shooter around so that the ball comes at the keeper from all angles.
- Make the shot go to the far wall.

Set Plays

A kick from the free kick spot on the red line is probably the most common set play. Occasionally, the kicker can shoot on goal, but in most cases, the kicker will need to make a direct pass or a pass off the back wall. It is advisable, then, to give the kicker both options as shown in Exhibit 11-12. Note the two defenders in a "wall" in front of the kicker.

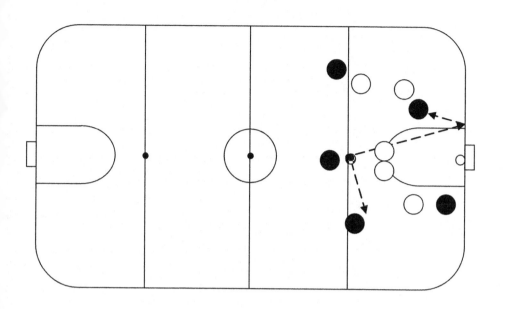

Exhibit 11-12

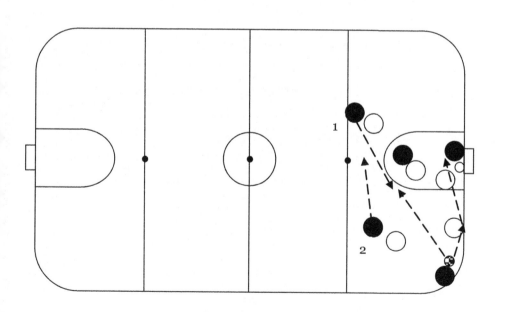

Exhibit 11-13

Other set plays, such as corner kicks, occur less frequently. Practicing set plays other than the free kick from the red line are at the discretion of the coach and may be limited by field time.

A corner kick set up is shown in Exhibit 11-13. The kicker should have at least two options. In the exhibit, the kicker can pass against the back wall and into traffic in the penalty area. Either of the two players in the penalty area can step around their defenders to make the one touch shot. The other option is to pass to player 1 making the move as player 2 is a decoy.

Summary of drills

The drills in this chapter can be performed in a structured practice in combination with traditional drills for improving dribbling, shooting, and passing. They can also be done in the few minutes of warm up time before a game. Either way, practicing the drills in this section is critical to sharpening the skills needed to excel in indoor soccer.

Conclusion

It is my hope that you learn *one thing* from this book. However, I don't know what that one thing is. Perhaps it is that indoor soccer is dramatically different from outdoor soccer, the best game system for your team, what to do in an odd man rush, how the keeper should release the ball, or something else.

You may learn more than one thing; I certainly hope so. But if you remember only one thing from this book, no matter what it is, and it helps improve your game, you will be a better player and I will have achieved my goal to help you.

To order additional copies, please contact:

BookSurge
www.booksurge.com
1-866-308-6235
orders@booksurge.com

Quantity discounts available for teams or leagues.

Made in the USA
Coppell, TX
25 September 2021